It's Time 4 GOD

To: JoAnn

God Bless You

Brenda Garner

TATE PUBLISHING
AND ENTERPRISES, LLC

Published by Tate Publishing & Enterprises, LLC
127 E. Trade Center Terrace | Mustang, Oklahoma 73064 USA
1.888.361.9473 | www.tatepublishing.com

Tate Publishing is committed to excellence in the publishing industry. The company reflects the philosophy established by the founders, based on Psalm 68:11,
"The Lord gave the word and great was the company of those who published it."

Published in the United States of America
ISBN: 978-1-63268-161-4
Religion / Christian Life / Inspirational
14.11.04

To God my Father, who continually shows his amazing love for me
To Jesus my Savior, who came and took my place on the cross

Acknowledgments

At every moment in my life, I can remember God walking quietly around me, putting people in place to work things out in my life. I am forever thankful for his abounding love, constant grace, and unconditional mercy. My mouth has a familiar phrase and rightfully so: 'Thank you God!'

Jesus took all the sins that I would ever commit, forgave me and then forgot them all. He came and made his home in my heart, and gave me a new place to call my home: 'heaven.' How could I ever *praise him* enough? I have gratitude for him loving me so much there is a constant song in my heart. This book can be full of nothing but thank you; and it is. However, it is a witness of how he moved on one person's behalf.

Thank you to my wonderful husband that encouraged me to write this, and my children Michelle and Michael who inspired me to share, and of course my entire family, love always!

Contents

Introduction

Experience his Love!

We have all encountered God at one time or another, but do we truly pay attention when he is moving people, places, and things so he can put us in position to receive all that he has for us? Let me encourage you to watch even the little things God does because he loves you 'Just that much!'

> God is magnificent; he can never be praised enough. There are no boundaries to his greatness. Generation after generation stands in awe of your work; each one tells stories of your mighty acts. Your beauty and splendor have everyone talking; I compose songs on your wonders. Your marvelous doings are headline news; I could write a book full of the details of your greatness.
>
> Psalms 145:3–6 (ESV)

These are true stories, and as you read, you will see how God moved in, around, and through one person's life.

Godly Women

Growing up in my home was always entertaining. There were four kids and my mom, and Mom was always working. Mom didn't have the time to keep up with all of us but Mom did the best she could. Being the strong-willed one, Mom was always patient with my attitude to be in charge. I always thought I was in charge, and my mom let me think that, while she controlled everything. We were in church every week, because we had a grandma that did not want us to miss out on hearing about Jesus, or maybe it was just mom's time away from us. We were all grateful that we had Grandma, and she enjoyed taking us places. We also liked being away from home since our stepdads were not exactly very nice to us. So anytime we had the opportunity to be at the park, at friends, or at church, we were there.

Now everyone should have a Grandmother like mine. She came over every weekend to take us to church, and she lived a life that showed everyone what love was all about. She never had an unkind word to say about anyone. She would welcome anyone into her house, and because she was from the older generation she had that gift of hospitality, where you felt you were at home.

She would ask you if you wanted a drink, and if you said 'no' she would ask if you wanted something to eat. If you said 'no' again, she would take you around her house until you took something—a trinket, a scripture verse, a piece of costume jewelry, or just something—that was just her generous spirit. One time my girlfriend came over to meet her for the first time, and I warned her that she would kiss her on the mouth. She said, "No way!" As soon as she walked in…'SMACK' right on the lips! Grandma loved everyone and it showed; she was my wonderful example of Jesus.

"Many women have done excellently, but you surpass them all" (Proverbs 31:29, English Standard Version).

What you're going to read next is what happened in just one life. If you pay attention, you can see God walking quietly through and doing what only he can do. Except for when I did things for God, my life was fairly routine. When I look back, I remember being so excited just going to Sunday school with my sister. We went to church every Sunday and had a wonderful Sunday school teacher, Mrs. Rich, who took us under her wing and seemed to be that permanent fixture in our lives. She was always encouraging and teaching us. She was there for our school events, weddings, and even the births of our children.

As I look back she truly was a gift from God. She never looked down on us, and she was always there when we needed a break from our lives at home. She fed us, threw parties for us, and spoke truth into our lives, even though we didn't know what it meant at the time. She was my Sunday school teacher from the time I was in fifth grade until I graduated from high school.

I was thankful to God for allowing her to stay with us through the entire process. God knew I needed someone extra special to help guide me through my life, and she definitely was that. Once again, thank you Jesus, for sending someone to us even when we did not know we needed her.

"But a woman who fears the LORD is to be praised" (Proverbs 31:30, ESV).

Never the Same

I remember a particular week when I was eleven years old, and I was happy because my church was having a revival. It was awesome—in church, every day, and dinner too. You see, as kids we would rather be in church as our stepdads would beat us and lock us out of the house without anything to eat all day long until Mom got home. I would go dumpster-diving in the back of the local grocery store for day-old donuts and such, which was sort of an adventure for me, but the church was a safe place. I just didn't realize it at the time.

One Tuesday, my sister and I were sitting on the second row of the church, and the pastor came and sat down next to us.

He said, "Now Brenda, you and Lacy pay attention to what this guest speaker is going to say. No passing notes, no talking, and you need to stay sitting right here!"

We both said, "Okay."

As soon as he left, we passed notes and whispered as we normally did. The young man got up and stood at the pulpit and started talking. Everything he said was noise to me except for, "You have a heavenly Father that loves you and will never leave you." Those words struck a chord in me and made me sit up and pay attention like being smacked with cold wet towel.

You see my mom had been married several times before I was ten years old, and all the men in mom's life said that they loved me, but when I got up in the morning they were gone. When this guy said I had a heavenly Father that loved me and would never leave me, he had my attention. I was really nervous and scared, and I couldn't wait for the service to end to talk to the young man. I felt the young man was speaking only to me; like I was the only one there, right beside me, right to my heart.

When would this service end, so I could get this *heavenly Father* he talked about? When they gave the invitation, I can't tell you how I got down there. I just took the first step, and I was there! Lacy was right behind me, ready to receive Jesus into her heart as well. I went down to the front, prayed, and accepted Jesus Christ as my *savior*. But the best thing about it was that I knew, from that moment on, that I had a Father that would never leave me and love me no matter what. I came to realize that whenever I needed God to be in my life—whether a friend, spouse, provider, healer, or comforter—my heavenly Father was that for me (God was always that for me).

From that point on, my life changed dramatically. I changed from being selfish, mean, and always bullying everyone around me to someone not afraid to be me. When Christ came in, I no longer had to be first; I didn't have to be in charge and I didn't have to win at any cost. It was just my heavenly Father loving me completely. God was working things out in me because at church camp that summer, I got the award for being a good sport. It was the only trophy I had ever won! Imagine, winning a trophy because God changed your heart. I truly was a winner!

"For God so loved the world, that he gave his only Son, that whoever believes in him should not perish but have eternal life" (John 3:16, ESV).

Truth Will Rule

I was in grade school and I had a difficult teacher. She couldn't be pleased no matter how hard you tried. This one particular day there were several of us that did not quite get our lessons done —okay we just did not do them. So for punishment, we had to stay in at recess. Dang! The only good thing out of school was recess and lunch. The teacher not only gave us our lessons to do, but she gave us another assignment as well.

She said that it was not being focused and getting things done, yuck! See what I mean, just downright mean! Not only did we have to do more work, but even if we got done, we were only allowed to lay our heads down on the table. She left the room with the echoes of, "I'll be back in a few minutes."

That should have been the right incentive to focus and not repeat the same mistake again, but, just as soon as she stepped out of the room, six boys started throwing pencils and paper and anything else they could get their hands on. They threw at each other and the ceiling in a radius that little boys can throw. Did they not hear the same thing I heard, she would be back?

I guess the boys thought they were immune from any punishment a teacher might impose, and, me, being the one that has to have no noise; I mean no noise—none, zip, zero, to be able to study. I looked up from my paper to tell the boys that they need to stop or they will get into trouble. It was a mistake on my part, and I became the new target of the thrown things. I'm trying to help them, and this is what I get!

The plot thickens as one boy threw his ruler at me, so I pick it up, not to throw it back to him, but to give it to the teacher when she came back. At that moment she walks back in and sees the mess, I mean, really what did she expect from young boys unsupervised, but the worse thing was she saw me with the ruler in my hand and thought I was fixing to throw it.

Guilty by association, and I must be the ringleader by her expression. She then looked at all of us, even though I was doing my work the whole time.

"All right, line up by the door, single file," she said, and I begin to wonder what was going to happen next. She took me first (the ringleader) out in the hallway and asked me what I was doing. I said I was doing my homework just like you said.

She then asked, "Brenda, why do you have a ruler in your hand." I told her someone threw it at me, and I was picking it up to give it to you just when you came back. She looked at me and said, "I don't believe you, bend over!" Bend over, what for. Then she said "grab your ankles." I got three smacks with a yardstick across my backside (Back then they could give you spankings without telling your parents). I didn't cry, but I did have tears coming out my eyes.

As I walked by the boy that threw the ruler at me, he lipped, "Sorry" so that no one heard him, but I didn't care. It wasn't the spanking I got that hurt me as much as she didn't believe what I told her. That hurt me to the inner child that was innocent and truthful that I wanted her to see in this situation, but she didn't. This was the second time I got a spanking in school. I never got another spanking after that. Both times it wasn't my fault, but no one was willing to listen. God showed me that He knew what I did and the truth, so I can hold my head high because He my Father in heaven saw *me*. Thank you, Father that you always know the truth, and one day everyone else will too.

John the apostle wrote, "…you shall know the truth, and the truth shall make you free" (John 8:32, ESV).

Angels Are Watching

Remembering back when I was younger, my grandma invited me and my sister over to spend the night. She had recently remarried and was living in a newer house. As we came over, she was talking quietly as she showed us around the house. It was very clean and everything was in its place. Her new husband Oliver walked into the room. He was drunk, and we were sitting on the couch. She then ushered us into another room.

In about ten minutes, we heard him yelling and screaming at grandma. He said, "I'm going to kill you." He then went into another room and grabbed a hammer. Grandma went running outside. I know because I heard the door slam and we were watching out the window. She went running down the street and knocking on doors asking anyone for help, because there was a man chasing her with the intent to kill her. When no one would answer the door, she ran behind a car and ducked down to hide. About that time, Oliver came around the car and raised his hand with the hammer in it, ready to hit her. Suddenly, another man came from out of nowhere and grabbed his arm. Oliver said, "I'm going to kill her." The man said, "NO, No you're not, leave her alone!"

Oliver turned, dropped the hammer, and went back into the house. Grandma had been in the fetal position with her hands covering her head. When she heard Oliver walking away, she stood up. She wanted to thank the man, who saved her, but he just vanished! He wasn't walking down the street—he didn't have time. He didn't run into a house, or jump into a time machine. We all had goose bumps because Grandma's angel was protecting her. I learned that day that I could completely trust him as my Great Shepherd. Thank you, Father, for allowing us to keep my grandma, she was such a blessing to us all.

God's word says, "He will never leave us or forsakes us" (Hebrews 13:5, ESV).

I Didn't Do It

When I was younger, I could remember being outside most of the time. I would rather be outside playing than inside the house even if it meant I wasn't going to get anything to eat. This particular evening, we sat down to eat, and I was hurrying to get outside. This was mostly because our backyard was right next to the woods, and I was thinking what fun I could have exploring it.

However, it was my time to do the dishes after dinner. I got everything done but one, really sticky mess of a pan. I knew it would take a year to clean it up, probably fifteen minutes in reality. I just didn't have the time! I needed to be outside, so I filled the pan up with water, stuck it under the cabinet, and told myself that I was going to come back later to finish cleaning it up.

It wasn't even fifteen minutes later that my mom called me and Lacy back into the house. She was holding 'the pan'. My heart sank. She looked at us both and said, "Who did this?"

Lacy quickly replied, "It wasn't me."

I followed with the same I didn't do it. Then my mom looked at Lacy and said, "It must have been you because Brenda never lies." I said nothing, hoping that she could see the lie all over my face. To no avail, Lacy kept on insisting it wasn't her, with judgment quick to follow. Lacy was whisked off to the bedroom and given a spanking. I felt awful, so much so that I started crying.

Mom said "what's wrong?" I said "mom it was me; and now Lacy is getting a spanking for something I did." She said, "You better go apologize to Lacy."

I told Lacy I was sorry. There's nothing I could do. I had no words that were good enough. She looked at me and said, "That's okay."

But I still felt bad, and my heart ached. It couldn't erase the damage I had already done. Mom didn't trust me anymore; Lacy was punished for something I did. I never got punished for anything! God gently reminded me that was exactly what he did for me. Even though he never did anything wrong he didn't mind taking my place. Thank you Jesus for showing me just a glimpse of what you did for me. Man, it hurt me to the core to think I did that. When it was all said, and done Jesus said, it's okay. Now that's love.

My Bike

I remember was when I was twelve years old when I was out riding my bike. You see my bike was a ten-speed custom bike made up from parts we got from the Salvation Army drop-off box. The handlebars were banana bars the seat was a banana seat, all on a ten-speed frame. Here's the kicker though, the ten-speed shifter didn't work, so you might be riding fast down a hill, and the chain would fall off—the resulting crash would give a whole new meaning to crash dummy.

Because it had no brakes, like everything else, we improvised using my shoes to drag the ground and stop. Maybe you were a crash dummy too; well it was what we had and I was grateful. One day the neighborhood kid drove up beside me on his fancy bike and started laughing at my bike.

I just looked at him and said, "That's okay; it gets me where I'm going".

Just a week later, I got seventy dollars for my birthday. I was rich and so excited. As I was thinking of the new bike I could buy now—you know the one with the gold handlebars and cushioned seat, I remembered what I had just learned in Sunday school. God points out that we need to honor him with first of our increase, and watch the blessing that comes from tithing.

So without a second thought of spending the money, I went to church and gave my first seven dollars as a tithe for the birthday money. I was so happy that I could finally give to God! It was amazing knowing that someone might come to know Jesus if I gave, a true blessing from God.

However, not thinking about it, when I gave the seven dollars it left me short of money to get that NEW BIKE I wanted, but it didn't take away the feeling I had when I gave to God. God was moving and one day the next week when I got home from school, there was a new ten-speed BIKE waiting for me. I asked my mom where the money came from. Mom said, "It was a present from your dad!"

Now forget that I have never met him, but he still sends both my sister and me money for a new bike. So I jumped on my bike and off I went. The kid that had made fun of me just a few days earlier came around the corner and saw my bike.

He said "WOW!" I just looked and smiled because I knew I had a better bike than him because my Father had my back. Thank you God for giving to me way more than I could ever give to you, you are so awesome!

Fish, Fish, and More Fish

We were at home on summer break, and we always managed to get into trouble with little effort. Mom was at work, and we were watching TV, one of the four channels we received over the TV antenna.

Trent and Mary, my little brother and sister, sat down in the living room and got into a fight, a repeated theme. Now as you know, I'm not one for interfering, so I didn't. The skill was to egg them on but not enough to get you in trouble; I was a master in that. Before I knew it, Trent had shoved Mary into the fish aquarium, as there were sixty fish and lots of water everywhere, I may have pushed too far.

They started arguing and saying, "You did it" and "no you did it". One of fish we had was named Hank. He was about as round as a tennis ball and about six inches long. There was about thirty gallons of water in the carpet. Who knew the carpet could soak up that much water so quickly. It can't! There was about three inches of water everywhere, the fish were flopping, and the kids were arguing, and I yelled, "Hey! Stop it! We need to get these fish in some water".

So the race was on. Bowls came out of the cabinets, as fast as popcorn popping. We were scooping up everything in sight and trying to make sure we didn't squash anything in the process. When it was all said and done, we had bowls that covered the kitchen table and bowls all over the kitchen countertops—about twenty in all. Then out of nowhere Mary looked at me and said, "Do you think your mom will notice?"

I said, "I'm not sticking around to find out." I am the oldest in the house, so you would think I would stand and face the music. But, no, we all left before mom got home. Mom told us later that she first stepped on the carpet and water came up between her toes. She then had to go rent a Shop-Vac to vacuum-up all the water and then figure out where to put the fish. I'm sure she was mad, but she never blew up at us. She just looked at us and said "let's just clean this all up."

To think we had such a kind, forgiving, and compassionate mother, and, yet, we never thanked her for all that she did for us. Thank you Father for giving us such a gracious mother who loved us in spite of everything we managed to ruin.

Thank you for letting her show us that we mattered more than the stuff! I guess I didn't push too far after all, or maybe like grace it covers a multitude of sin, even the fishy kind.

I Hate Doing Dishes

There was a night called date night. This was time for Mom and Dad to dance away the stress of work, even though there was the hint that children may have been a consideration. We loved that they liked dancing and going out together, and of course we couldn't afford babysitters (might have been no one would take the job), so the house was ours to do as we pleased, within reason, and time to clean everything up of course. Mary had about four or five friends over for a slumber party. Lacy was in her room, doing whatever older sisters do. I didn't know where Trent was, but it didn't matter. I was listening to Mary tell the girls in the bedroom downstairs that at midnight there was going to be a BOOGIE MAN to come and get them.

Now, you know, I couldn't let this go, so I sprang into action. I went upstairs to mom's room and got a trench coat, ski mask, and black gloves. I then went to the kitchen, got a butcher's knife, went outside, crawled under the garage door, and waited until Mary announced it was midnight.

I heard Mary say, "You only have one minute and the BOOGIE MAN is going to get you."

Now these girls were already shaking, but Mary wasn't. She didn't know what was coming. At the pronouncement of midnight, I grabbed the door and tried to open it, but Mary had latched the door with a chain (I was not deterred); I slid my arm with the coat, glove, and knife in the door and yelled, "ROAR!" The girls screamed, pushed Mary back down on the bed, and proceeded to find sanctuary in Lacy's room. Mary got so scared that she was crying and screaming. I will admit that I have an off sense of humor at times, but I was laughing my head off as I came back into the house. I found the girls huddled in the bathroom crying and hugging Lacy.

They were all yelling, "I want to go home." Lacy said to me, "What did you do?" my reply was, "Mary started it; she was telling them the BOOGIE MAN was coming to get them, and I didn't want her to lie." All Mary could do was to try and comfort the girls and shake her head in disapproval. I then realized that the girls may tell on me and action was needed.

I told the girls I would take them all to Seven-Eleven and get them and an ICEE with the biggest smile I could muster. The kids said, "NO, I just want to go home." So I stepped it up and said, "Okay, then how about an ICEE *and* a candy bar if you won't tell on me?"

They all finally agreed. So at midnight, pitch-dark, rattled girls, and hope of quiet mouths, we all started walking to Seven-Eleven. I was walking fast and the little girls couldn't keep up. They were yelling, "Stop. We can't keep up!" So, I stopped in the middle of the road and folded my hands looking at them in disgust. All of a sudden they all started running by me, and then the "old me" kicked-in. I didn't want them to beat me going to the store. They just happened to be on a very busy street and a car was driving by. I sprang into action and yelled, "Duck he's got a gun."

They all dropped to the ground, and I ran around them. They just laid there shaking and crying AGAIN. Needless to say I spent over seven dollars that night, which was a lot back then. When I got home, the bargaining began. Mary said, "I won't tell if you do my dishes for a week," then Lacy chimed in and said, "I won't say anything if you do my dishes for a week."

I hate doing dishes more than anything else in the world, and everyone in my house knew it including my mother. It was about the third week into me doing the dishes. My mom came around the corner and said, "dishes again?" I said, "I like doing the dishes." She then looked at me and said "I don't know what you did, but it must have been good."

Thank you, Father, for a mom that showed me mercy and grace even though I never seemed to show it to people around me.

Baby Brother

My sister Lacy was always compassionate especially with animals. This one particular day she had notice a baby bird that had fallen out of the tree with an injured leg. When she went to get the bird, the mother bird swooped down and dive bombed Lacy. Lacy grabbed the baby bird and brought it in the house. Lacy doctored the little leg up and waited for it to get better.

Now we had the task of who was going to take it in the backyard. So I think Trent, our smaller brother, would be perfect. We grabbed Trent and told him to go take the little bird and set him down in the middle of the yard. Trent goes out the back door, and is about half way into the yard, when all of a sudden there isn't just one bird but there were two birds dive-bombing him. They were relentless, even so far as hitting him on his head. Now Trent was either traumatized or unaware of what the birds were doing as he just stood there. We yelled out of the bedroom window, "Set him down, and set him down." Finally, after being hit four or five times by the flying birds, Trent set the baby bird down.

The birds, however, didn't seem to care that the baby bird was put down on the ground, as they kept coming after him, swoop, hit him again, and again. Then we screamed, "Run, Trent, run." The image of Trent finally running reminded us of Forrest Gump being told run the Forrest run, arms pumping, legs moving, and head high as the birds swooped down, time and time again. I would like to say that we didn't laugh, but I can't. Lacy and I were laughing our heads off. Trent was running in the house by now and said, "did you see that?" I offered him a stick of bubble gum for the show.

We sure did enjoy having Trent around especially because he never seemed to mind anything we did to him. Thank you, Father for having such a sweet little brother; I'm sure Mom was glad that at least one of her kids was!

Unstable and Unable

Trent was excited as he was fixing to go visit his real Dad for the weekend. He looked at everyone especially me and said, "Now, I do not want anyone messing with my skateboard while I'm gone."

He couldn't have been talking to me, because I lived on this huge hill and it just screamed for anyone to ride down it, whether on a bike, skates, BIG WHEEL, and yes, and even a skateboard. He wasn't gone fifteen minutes when I grabbed that bad boy and went for a ride. I got as high up as you could get on the hill and let it fly. I was about halfway down the street when I hit a bump; I flew off of the board and rolled for what felt like was about six houses. I scraped up my knees, my feet (I was barefoot) my elbows, and my face. I got up and kicked the board. I was going to be really mad until I saw that the wheels were fixed to fall off. Trent had fixed it so that if anyone rode his skateboard the wheels would fall off and was probably chuckling as to which one of us girls would take the bait. I guess I had that coming for all the times I had gotten him and he never did anything about it. So history repeated itself that day. David defeated Goliath and I didn't ride his board ever again!

Leave Me Alone

My sentence of almost a month of dishes was very nearly up. I was ready for more. I was over at my friend's house, Deanne, visiting. Deanne was very insecure about her looks. She had acne; she was awkward and never quite fit in. She was sitting in her bedroom talking on her phone; she had her own number. Back in the 1970s, phones were attached to the wall, so she only had one choice if she wanted to talk on the phone, sit by it or not talk.

She had asked for the phone for Christmas, and her parents happily gave it to her. I didn't know anyone else with their own phone or number, so this was a big deal to me. There weren't any wireless phones yet, so she was pretty much in her room all the time talking to her friends. Then one specific day her mom was at work, and she had left Deanne and me in charge.

What was she thinking? Anyway it was Josh, Deanne's little brother, and I. I was sitting in the living room, and all of a sudden I hear Deanne screaming, "GET OUT, GET OUT, GET OUT!"

I came running down the hall, and Josh was singing a song, only putting his own words to it…"nana, nana, nana, nana…nana, nana, nana, nana, ending with Zit woman!" Deanne hadn't removed the phone from her ear so; whoever was on the other end was surely getting an ear full. I told Josh to leave her alone, so he went back into his room, and I went back to the living room. About three minutes later I heard Josh kick open the door and acted like he had a machine gun—pointing his finger at Deanne and pretending to shoot at her face. Deanne, still on the phone, was yelling "GET OUT, GET OUT, GET OUT!"

I ran down the hall and grabbed Josh and told him to stop it. He said "I have to go to a friend's house." I was glad he would be gone and the house would be quiet again. But then I got a brilliant idea and thought to call my friend, I told him to sing the song like Josh did, because she was off the phone. He could call in and sing it to her when she answered the phone. I thought it would be funny, so when she answered the phone, after about ten seconds, she starts screaming, "Josh I hate you!"

She didn't know it was someone else, and I was laughing my head off. A few minutes later I heard someone screaming, but this time it wasn't Deanne, it was Josh. I came running down the hall. Deanne was in the bathroom, and Josh was bent over the bathtub washing his hair. She was holding him down and hitting him in the back.

I yelled, "Deanne, stop, stop, stop." She said, "He isn't ever going to talk about me again." All the while she was hitting him as hard as she could on his bare back. Then she let up. Now, I have to say, anyone can reach their boiling point, and Deanne had reached hers. While Josh's back must have been sore, Deanne had been emotionally broken. We had picked on her and made her feel less than who she was. The damage lasted a lot longer for her. Josh had a mark that would stay with him for a while, but it was nothing compared to how insignificant we made her feel.

Father, forgive me when I don't show compassion, she was broken, and what's even worse, we added to her pain.

"Be gracious to me, O God, according to Thy Loving-kindness; According to the greatness of Thy compassion blot out my transgressions" (Psalms 51:1, ESV).

Affecting Lives

I was visiting a nursing home with my pastor. I was probably around fifteen years old. When we walked in, there was this lady, who was just lying there staring at the wall. It had over 150 pictures on it. She was just staring at them. Then my pastor introduced me to the woman, Mrs. Cook. I sat down as they visited for a little while and said good-bye. Then we left. I found out through their conversation that she was paralyzed from the neck down. When we got ready to leave, I said to my pastor what a miserable existence.

He said, "Oh no, Brenda you've got it all wrong. Remember all those pictures on the wall?"

I said "yes."

"Every day, Mrs. Cook, prays for each and every one of those people on that wall. We add new pictures all the time. In the kingdom of God she is a mighty warrior. She is affecting more lives than we will ever now. She touches heaven every day with her prayers. You can't look at a person and say whether or not they are valuable because they don't look like everyone else."

I was choked up and crying because I thought less of this lady because of her appearance. Father, forgive me for not seeing the value you do in everyone. Everyone can make a difference in their world, and it's in their weaknesses you make them strong. Help me to be mighty in the kingdom of God based on who you are, not on what I think I am.

"…Do not look on his appearance or on the height of his stature, because I have rejected him. For the LORD sees not as man sees: man looks on the outward appearance, but the LORD looks on the heart" (1 Samuel 16:7, ESV).

Not Another Test

School tests, yuck! If you are like me, whenever the teacher said there would be a test the next day, panic would set in. I was probably the worst for waiting until the last moment to study. At this particular time, I hadn't even gotten time to study—from practicing basketball, and other homework I was pretty much done for the day. The next day I knew that the test would be right after lunch, so I skipped lunch and hung out right outside the history room, so I could have as much time to study as I could. This test was going to be true or false. So, as I was sitting there (light bulb), I could study for all the false answers. You see we had a pre-quiz the day before, and it was true and false. So I could study all the wrong answers, and the rest would be true—brilliant, right? Now, I really didn't learn anything from it, but I did ace the test, in fact I was the only one.

The teacher came up to me after class and asked what I did to be the only one to ace the test. I told her the truth, how I figured out how to get better odds at passing tests. She thought it was brilliant, but I was still not through, I was going to be the first one to give an oral report with visual aids.

She said "the opportunity to learn is immeasurable." I said, "I see that." Once again, thank you, Father for providing a way out, but not without a price.

"Study to show thyself approved unto God, a workman that needs not to be ashamed, rightly dividing the word of truth"(2 Timothy 2:15, ESV).

Great Physician

There I was going into basketball at the age of fifteen, which is pretty unheard of since most of the girls had started in middle school. One day we were at another school. It wasn't a regular game, but we did win the game. Unfortunately, half way into the game, as I tried to cut between two girls, my body did, but my knee didn't. I tore the cartilage in my knee and was headed to the hospital.

They told me I wouldn't be walking for six weeks after the surgery, and wouldn't be able to run for three or four months. I was worried after they gave me the news and felt the need to ask God to bring me through this. After the surgery, I was in the hospital for three days, and, man, my knee felt weird and sore. I left the hospital, and they said that I would be coming back in two weeks to get the stitches out.

I told them, "Sure, but not with these crutches." They just smiled and said, "We'll see!" As soon as I got home, I had the confidence to stand and move around. So I just started using weights to get back into shape, and thanked God every day for improving my knee.

After two weeks, I walked back into the doctor's office, and they were shocked. Then less than four weeks later I was running again. You see the difference between what they said, and who I knew, was all the difference. I thank you, God, for giving me the confidence to take those first steps of faith, and continue until I was right where you wanted me. You see, I know the Great Physician, and he always has a good report.

We Gave Out of Our Need

It was my senior year in high school, and I had played basketball for three years. Our team was unbeatable. They elected me to be the team chaplain, so I got to pray before every game. It was an honor, and I never took it lightly. About two weeks left to go in the season, God had put it on both my sister and my heart that we needed to step up and help our mom with the finances for our family.

She struggled for as long as I can remember to help provide for us. She was dating again, and we didn't want any more pressure on my mother to feel like she had to marry quickly to provide for us. Lacy and I told mom that Lacy would help pay for the utilities, and I would buy the food. With four kids, the food went out the door as soon as it came in. So with only two weeks left, I quit the team. They still ended up taking State.

I was proud of them, but grateful I could be of more help to my family. Mom never did get married again; she never had to. My sister and I worked for three years helping Mom out. That's all it took for her to get enough promotions and raises on her job to be in a place where she didn't need to depend on others any longer. The entire team never knew about what we had done. It was sometime later, when one of my best friends in school came up to me and said, "I really admired what you and your sister did for your family. You had a choice to make, and you made the best one. Even though we all got medals, you chose what was more important."

I smiled and told her thank you.

Thank you, God for allowing us to make a difference by changing our world more than we could ever know.

"Give and it will be given to you. Good measure, pressed down, shaken together, running over, will be put into your lap. For with the measure you use it will be measured back to you" (Luke 6:38, ESV).

Just Call Me "Crash"

As my senior year was approaching, my mom informed me that I would need to get my driver's permit. I protested because I never wanted a driver's license. The fear of driving was a fear that caused anxiety and sweat to form on my hands. You see I was eighteen, moving to an apartment, with too many friends that would take me anywhere. Since I was going to be living ten more miles away, I had to get a license and be independent. So, not only do I have to get a license, but buy a car too. I took my written test and passed it, but only by one right answer. If I had missed anymore I would have flunked. Then I had to do the driving part, which I ran over the cones. They told me to come back in a week, yuck!

My mom wasn't too happy about it because she had to take off work to take me to the test. The next week I passed. It was up to me to find a car, and I did a 1970 Chevy Impala. I got it for $700 and had enough money saved to get insurance. I was off and running, but here is the problem—I was given a driver's license and had only driven a car ten minutes in my whole life. Experience was not in my corner, and neither was time, school was starting in just three weeks. I remember taking one of my sister's friends home one morning, and as I was coming out of the parking lot, when I saw a car coming. Instead of pushing the brake to stop, I hit the gas, and sure enough SMACK! I hit the car. The driver was very nice because he knew I was so nervous. The guy told me he tried to get out of the way, by running up on the curb. That only ended him up with a flat tire on top of everything else. My sister runs home, three blocks away, and gets my mom.

Mom comes around the corner and as she get near she said "I hope you know your insurance will pay for his car but not for yours. You will have to drive it looking like this."

I said "Okay." They then helped me pull my fender out away from the tire, and I was off and running. A few weeks later I was chasing one of my friends down the local drag when he darted around one car, and because I was so busy paying attention to him I never saw the car in front of me. SMACK I hit the truck in front of me, NOT AGAIN! I gave him my information, and he said he would call the next day. When I got home I told my mom that I hit another car. She asked about his information and I told her I couldn't get it.

She asked "Why not?"

"His breath was so bad that I couldn't get close to him."

She said, "What do you mean?"

I said, "he was throwing beer cans, and other stuff out of his truck and when he talked to me his breath made me sick. I didn't dent it or anything, all that was done was the bumper was shoved in about an inch."

The next day his dad called and said they were going to report it to the insurance. My mom told him that it was okay, but we would also report that his son was drinking and driving. The guy told my mom to hang on for a moment. You could hear him yelling at his son through the phone. Then he came back on and told my mom that would be okay, we would take care of it. I am not sure why I was protected from not having to pay for the little damage, but I was sure that God wanted to let his dad know he drank. God was watching over us both. When I got to work all the kids heard that I had gotten into another wreck, in less than six weeks. They all started calling me "CRASH." Yep you guessed, my nickname stuck. It probably wasn't two weeks later, on same road but on a different direction, I was looking in my rearview mirror when I looked up I hit the gas instead of the brake again, nuts! This poor guy had just fixed his muscle car in order to sell it.

He got out of the car and asked if I was okay?

I said sure. He said, "Well, just follow me over to my apartment. It's just a block away." When I got there, he invited me in. I stood in the middle of his living room as we talked. I told him that I would pay for the damage. All I can do is pay you everything I make for the next few months, but I promise I will pay you back.

He then looked at me and then looked at his bedroom and said, "Well, if you will sleep with me I will forget everything."

I said "NO way. Do I do that kind of stuff?"

He must have then realized what he said. He then said "I'm sorry I don't know why I said that, please forgive me, and just forget it. I will take care of it."

I never heard from him again. The sad thing was, I know, I probably did $3500 worth of damage on his car.

Thank you, God, for protecting me and helping me to be a person of integrity, so that even when things are bad I don't have to compromise my values. I could go on, but I will keep it short I ended up hitting three more cars. After having six wrecks in my first six months of driving, I finally figured out why I was hitting everyone. Someone told me when I first started driving to keep an eye on my rearview mirror, so that's what I did.

I wondered why I kept hitting everyone in the back. I had taken them literally. No, I'm not blonde. I also figured out what was the brake and what was the gas. Oh, by the way, my car never looked any worse, because I kept hitting it in the same place. I drove the car, dents and all, for four years.

Thank you, Lord for showing me that no amount of pushing will make you ready for something you're not. Thank you, for watching over me through the long process of finally figuring it all out. Especially for seeing in me what no one else could?

"And I am sure of this, that he who began a good work in you will bring it to completion at the day of Jesus Christ" (Philippians 1:6, ESV).

People, Places, and Pranks

As you can tell by the previous stories, I was somewhat of a practical joker—mostly at the expense of others. I liked to use shaving cream, and shoe polish on everyone's cars and when I say everyone…I mean everyone! One night I had an idea. Now, you know, at this time in my life I wasn't exactly using the brains God gave me. Everyone was working but me. We all worked at this huge grocery store with twenty-five checkout lanes. I decided it was time to get everyone's car while they were working. It was dark and they couldn't see me, plus most of them parked away from the front of the store to leave parking for customers.

I got everyone except the one guy who got on my nerves. He was always preaching, and he annoyed me, so I wasn't about to waste my shoe polish on him—that will show him. Since I knew they would be looking for anyone that did it, I did my own car, too, and hid in it when they came looking, sneaky, huh. Sure enough I had about ten cars at my house after work, beating on the door and yelling. Come on, Noodles, we know you're in there. Come on out! Just then one of the other boys said "hey look, someone got her car too, so it wasn't her!"

They left and I was spared the money it was going to take to clean thirty-two cars. The next day all the guys were hanging around the front doors and wasn't for sure why until the preacher boy showed up. They grabbed him and said we guess you're the one that got everybody's car last night.

He said "I don't know what you're talking about."

They said everyone's car got shoe polished but yours. They dragged him into the stockroom; shoe polished him and then threw him in the freezer. He was okay, but I wasn't. Someone else got what I should have gotten. I was really nice to the preacher boy after that, but it wasn't for the right reason. Father, forgive me for not being a true friend that someone could trust in.

Egg-citing Times

While driving around with my friend Emma, we decided to drive by work. Silly, how when we are at work we can't wait to get away, but when we are off we want to be there. Well, we were driving through the parking lot when I saw one of my arch enemies. He was the boss's assistant known as 'PET'. He was the owner's pet; the boss was a woman, who would do anything for him, even though he was rude to her, and everyone around him.

As we drove by, we began to taunt him, "Want a dog biscuit Pet?"

Then we would drive off and come back with yet another insult. The reason it was easy to torment him was he was working outside with the car loaders. A car loader would take a number, and when you drove up, he would load the groceries in your car.

As we came around again the owner of the store was standing with her 'pet'. Emma and I were still egging him on by driving slower and slower. We got really close on the next pass, and the "pet" yells, "get her!" All the car loaders, about eight of them, started throwing eggs.

Some came in the window, some hit me, some hit Emma, and most covered the car pretty thoroughly. We hit the gas and made a mad dash to the carwash where another friend was washing his car. When he saw my car, he took the hose and started washing mine off. All the while Emma was laughing hysterically. I was yelling at her to quit laughing, but the more I did, the more she just laughed. Several of the kids got off work to hear about how the owner gave the "Pet" eggs to get me. The war had just begun.

The other car loaders egged me on by telling me to get back at him, so I was in! Really, you think this was enough, but not for me. The kids told me where to meet them to get to his house later that evening. We were at the corner waiting for everyone to arrive. All of a sudden there were about ten kids that came running around the corner, and they had water balloons. It was a double cross! They were all aimed at me and my car. I stepped out and they all dive bombed me. More laughter from Emma the neighborhood giggle box. She was sitting in the car, as they were soaking me and her; she didn't care she was having fun. So I jumped in the car and started chasing them. Yes, with my car! They were running like ants. After a while I couldn't find any of them, so I decided to go back to Emma's house and change clothes. We told her little sister to watch outside to make sure to protect my car if they came by. Sure enough, a few minutes later her little sister starting yelling. We ran outside to see what's going on. Sure enough the eggers came by and instead of egging my car they egged her. Dang! Spoiled again! I jump into the car and start chasing them down again. By this time I'm serious. I'm taking them down. When I catch up with them, they are all in front of the "Pet's" house. We come to a truce, and end up being the best of friends. Guess misery loves company. Thank you, God for not only getting what I deserved, but getting new friends in the process. I can laugh now, because if I hadn't started egging, I might not have gotten egged. Thank you, God that you don't let me get away with things that shape my character.

Following in His Footsteps

We were told in my senior year that we were going to have to move from the north side of town to the south side. We were not happy about that because we were living in a very nice neighborhood, and we would be moving to a lower middle class neighborhood. The first day we were there, however, the neighbors came out and introduced themselves. That was very unusual since we had lived on the north side for seven years, and no one ever introduced themselves. So, guess this place must not be all that bad.

We met the girl that lived across the street and even her boyfriend. As we started talking we learned that the boyfriend of the girl had a mother that had the same last name as a man my mom was dating. We came to find out that the boy's mother was married to this man, who was dating my mom. Talk about a small world. To think we would move twenty miles to the other side of town, and move right next door to the man who was dating my mom. As soon as my mom found out, she informed his mother. Who then had some long conversations with her husband, their marriage didn't make it. Neither one of them knew Jesus, so they had nothing to build a marriage on. It didn't end there. A young man, Jack, who was very fond of me, asked me out but I didn't trust him. I kept my distance. Jack would come over and we would sit in front of my house, and my mom would flip on the lights for me to come in after about fifteen minutes. Jack had a bad reputation, and we weren't letting our guard down for one minute.

One night Jack and I talked a little longer than usual. Mom must have gotten interested in a movie or something. Anyway as we talked, I told Jack about this guy that came to see the lady across the street. His name was Ted. I said he isn't fooling anyone because he drives up in several different vehicles, and he thinks we don't know it's him.

Jack said, "Hang on just a minute, would you please get in the car because I need to show you something." He took me down the road about four miles and turned the corner and said are these the cars? Sure enough it was every car, van, truck, caddy, Chevy, and a Dodge.

I said, "Yes, yes, they are!" He said that's where I live and they belong to my dad. He drove me home, and I could tell he was about to cry, but he didn't say a word after that. The next day Ted walked over to me as I was cleaning shoe polish off of my car, and he said, "If you think you're going to marry my son you have another thing coming. He is already dating someone else he is going to marry."

I didn't say anything out of respect, but I thought *like father like son.* Some years later I connected with Jack again, he was not what he had been in high school. He had accepted Jesus as his savior and was living for the Lord. He didn't want his life to end up like his dad's. However, he did have a wonderful Father he came to know and love that was a perfect example for him. Thank you, Father that our beginning doesn't have to define our end.

"Come, you who are blessed by my Father, inherit the kingdom prepared for you from the foundation of the world" (Matthew 25:34, ESV).

Lemon or Lemonade

My sister Lacy was graduated and getting married. She didn't want the expense of paying for this Yellow Oldsmobile Starfire. Look it up you probably don't remember them because they probably only made ten. These cars had so many issues with them they were almost as bad as Ford Pintos, if you're old enough to remember those. Lacy couldn't take the car, so I took over the payments for her and got a new car in the process.

My sister Mary was learning to drive and took every opportunity to get some driving time whenever she could. One day after work she had come up to see if I would take her home. I decided to let her drive me home. When she got in the car, I reminded her to make sure and pull forward enough not to hit the median since we were parked beside it. She didn't listen, and a second later, Bump! Bump! I yelled, "Mary, I told you watch out!" Then as she was finishing getting over the one curb, she turned and hit another median. I yelled again, "What are you doing? STOP the car."

She gathered herself and proceeded to drive out of the parking lot. She came to the stop and as she turned she didn't allow enough room to make the turn. Guess what happened next? She ran over the curb again! Now this was the little car that didn't have the clearance like the big ole Impala did, so I grabbed the wheel and brought it back to the street.

It's then that she came to another stop sign and proceeded to turn right onto the main street when the fun began, when she began to turn right on to Main Street, the driver's door flung open!

Dang driver's door, it had done that to me several times. Mary screamed and started to grab the door and shut it. As she did, she turned the wheel, and you can guess what happened next. Yes that's right she ran right up onto another curb.

"Dang it!" I'm yelling again, telling her to just get out, and I would drive home. Needless to say, she never asked me to take her for a driving lesson again. I couldn't blame her. I wasn't prepared to teach her. I can't imagine her ever wanting help from me again. Believe this or not, I am wonderful at teaching young people how to drive, patient, kind, and thoughtful. I wish I could have shown my sweet, caring, and loving sister all those attributes instead of yelling and criticizing her. Forgive me, Father, for not showing the wonderful example she always tried to show to me. Thank you, God for my sister who loved me in spite of me.

"Love bears all things, believes all things, hopes all things, endures all things" (1 Corinthians 13:7, ESV).

Never Mix Business

Wow, turning eighteen, becoming an adult, and all that it implied. Best of all I could exercise my right to do what I was not allowed to do before— no curfew, legal age to drink, and even some dance clubs. It was 1978 and disco was big for all my friends. To honor the occasion, I decided to throw myself a birthday party, a whim, a fancy, I was eighteen, and an adult.

Mom gave me strict guidelines to follow, so I could have my adult party. I asked people from work, from school, and personal friends. I was grown up, so I asked my mom to get us stuff for strawberry daiquiris, the 'drink of adults'. Mom knew I wasn't a big fan of liquor (I hated the way it smelled); in fact, I had to look up the spelling, even now, darn dictionary takes so long.

I never thought much of it, but all my friends said I should celebrate and take a drink. Somehow on the night of the party, my mom also gave me the use of the house. My sisters and brother would spend the night at someone else's home, and my mom at her friend's house, which just happened to be next door being able to hear and quickly return. I was ready for my big party.

As my friends arrived, they all went to different areas of the house. The people from work stayed in the living room, school stayed in the kitchen, and other friends stayed in the patio out back. No one even associated with each other. It was the oddest party I had been to, and it was mine, the adult. I drank my daiquiri and thought this tasted strange. I realized that things sounded slower, and I felt warmer and a little sleepy.

Later I took a sip of another one, my badge of adulthood, still hating the smell, and darn if my head started hurting. Yep, I was done, really done, and my head hurting and before I knew it I was asleep. I woke up the next morning, and somehow in the evening, my dull friends bought beer, as there were cans all over the house. It was just then my mom walked into the room at the same time I did, and she asked "What happened last night?"

I told her what happened. Mom listened as we cleaned up the mess. I never really desired to drink; it was a social thing that everyone said I had to try. Why? It wouldn't make me any older. It most assuredly didn't make me smarter, and for the first time in my life, I wasn't sure about being an adult, or drinking, or my not needing my mom. I woke up not knowing what went on that evening. So how did this add to my life? It was at this time I ask God to take away any desire for alcohol. I realized at a very young age that I never want to do anything that didn't allow me to be able to focus on God. Thank you, Father, for being my one and only desire! That even in the mistakes we can find grace and the good for those that choose to love God.

"If you do well, will you not be accepted? And if you do not do well, sin is crouching at the door. Its desire is for you, but you must rule over it" (Genesis 4:7, ESV).

Row, Row, Row Your Canoe

A group of us from work decided that we wanted to go floating down the Illinois River. It started out being just the four of us, but by the time we actually went there it was a dozen. We thought the more the merrier. So we had a caravan of cars driving up to the river. When we got there everyone had an ice chest full of food and drinks to take us through the whole day. Let's face it. We were cheap and had to save money wherever we could. As we checked in, the man made us all give deposits for the canoe. Seriously, it was $25, and all I had left for gas to get back on. He told all of us to watch our canoes, that when we brought them back, we would get our deposit.

For clarification I asked him again. So does that mean if I don't bring the canoe back I won't get my money back? He said, "Yes." They took us all up the river and dropped us ten miles up. That's what we paid for eight hours. As we put our canoes in the river I saw the water was really low.

Since I had never been, I asked the guys what happens when you get stuck. Yes I asked I wanted to make sure. They said, "Well you get out and drag it to a place that the water is deeper. What?"

When they said float down the river I wasn't expecting to have to get in and out of the canoe. Before I knew it they all had jumped in the canoes and took off.

I thought, *we were supposed to stay together?* I grabbed Denise and told her, let's go or they will leave us. I never realized that when they dropped us off we would end up in the same place we parked our cars. Now, why I didn't figure that out was beyond me, but this left me nervous. The trip was fun at first, but the guys could care less if we were okay or not. I decided I wasn't going to take them anymore if I went on a trip again. The water was smooth and easy to maneuver for the first three miles. Then as we came around this one bend the water was moving faster. I thought this is great no more paddling just sitting back and letting the water take you. Wrong! Do you know that if you just let the water take you where it wants, it runs you into trees, rocks, banks, and believe it or not, other canoes?

We quickly jumped into action using the paddles to keep the trees from smacking us upside the head. We used the paddles to keep from running the canoe into other people, people—we didn't even know. When we hit other people's canoes they would get upset and shove us away from them. What a ride as the canoe would get shoved and whirl around. Now, I am thinking, *This is fun?* Now, the boys were nowhere in sight. I figured that at least the only other girl would have stuck around to make sure we were okay, NOT!

We did manage to come across a couple who showed us how to steer the silly thing, and that would have been helpful at the beginning of our journey. But we were grateful for any help and it did make it better. The water was coming even more swiftly, and there were more turns to try and get through. As we rounded the next corner, there was a tree limb hanging down. It hit Denise and knocked her out of the canoe, and as she fell out it turned the whole canoe over. I was under the water stuck under the canoe, which was in about ten feet of water. Now, all I could remember was I didn't want to lose the silly canoe —or I wouldn't get my money back. Yes, all this went through my head while underwater and losing my breath. I was holding on for dear life to the canoe, and then realized I was trapped. Suddenly I felt someone grab my shirt and pull me to the top. I gasped and grabbed him tightly. I never saw the man's face because I was too busy hugging him. He never said anything to me, but I said lots to him. "Thank you! Thank you! Thank you!"

Then I turned around and remembered the canoe, oh my God where did it go? I looked up and as I did, I saw Denise holding on the canoe on the riverbank. Whew! I turned around and the man was gone. I never saw him again, wouldn't have known if I did, because I never saw his face. It did give me chills when I thought about it later, because he was there to save me and, then he's gone! I asked Denise if she saw anything, no she said I saw you standing up after the canoe floated to me. Thank you, thank you, thank you, God, for sparing my life. For showing me I was more important than the $25 I would have lost. Sometimes, we fear one thing so much; we lose sight of immediate danger. Thank you, Father, that I never want to hang on to something to tight it chokes the life out of me.

"But I call to God, and the LORD will save me" (Psalms 55:16, ESV).

Divine Destiny

Another time, I knew God had quietly walked around me, when I was eighteen. Tori, an awkward girl in the neighborhood that was about two or three years younger than I was, followed me everywhere I went. I couldn't get rid of her, but after a while I didn't mind her being there. I was getting ready to move from one apartment to another when Tori showed up out of nowhere. I was busy, and didn't want to be bothered. As she approached me, I was somewhat annoyed. I had a time schedule and didn't need or want to stop for any reason. Tori was a twin and wanted her own identity. Her father was a police officer. Since she was really never an overachiever, she got less and less attention. I probably wasn't the best person she could have gone to if she wanted someone to console her.

As she stepped up to me, the look on her face was very hopeless. I stopped for a minute to see what was wrong, and she started to talk to me about all the crazy things that were in her life. She talked about how she didn't care about anything anymore and was ready to leave. I asked her where she was going. She said it doesn't matter because no one will miss me anyhow. I immediately stopped her and said, are you kidding me? You have a lot of people that care about you.

She said, "Oh really? Seriously, I'm not the smartest one." My parents constantly fight about me. "I would be better off not even being here. Let's face it Brenda I bug you, you really don't want me around either."

Wow, I might have felt it, but I didn't realize it came across that way. I wasn't going to let her do anything hastily, so I sat down on the hood of my car, and we talked. This was God doing what he had to do, so one person would have someone to listen to her. Then God took over, he reminded me that I needed to tell her about his amazing love and what he did for her.

I said, "There is someone that understands where you are coming from."

I told her Jesus was rejected by everyone, and he was still willing to lay his life down for you. Jesus knew you before you were born, and knew everything you would do and he still took your sin. All you have to do is ask for forgiveness, accept him into your heart, and make him the Lord of your life.

Then I said, "Tori you have an amazing future, and God wants to use you to reach others. You know what it is like to be rejected. Wouldn't you like to know how it feels to be completely loved?"

We bowed our heads, and she prayed and accepted Jesus as her savior. She was crying and smiling at the same time. It was the first time I had the privilege to lead someone in the prayer of salvation. To think I couldn't be bothered with this young lady, and yet she saw something in me that she wanted. She told me that she was getting ready to go take a bottle of pills and end it all that night.

That shook me up. I was nervous and ashamed at the same time. To think if I hadn't taken the time for her, she would have ended it. Thank you, God for allowing Tori to see what you see in her. We became even better friends, and after college, she became a teacher where she affected many lives. I thank you Jesus for allowing her to see you, even in a dirty vessel like me.

Love Without Limits

I remembered when I first started to date. While over his house, and wanting to impress his mother Lisa, I started a conversation. I talked about everything and the weather. She asked what it was I did at the store. I begin to tell her I worked at the tobacco counter. Now, you might think this was weird since I don't smoke or ever did. Wait, I did smoke once when I was in the first grade. I was on my way to school, and I saw a cigarette lit on the ground. I picked it up and took a puff, and choked all the way home. I never wanted to do that again.

I proceeded to tell her that I worked with this witch of a person. I told her that she was so mean, and hateful to all the customers. Also, that she wore way too much makeup and even curled up her eyebrows. It made her eyes look awful. She just listened, and I told her the next time she came into the store, I would show her who I was talking about. It was probably three weeks later when Lisa came into the store.

When I saw her, I went up to her and told her to be sure and come see the witch lady. She was working today. She said okay, and went shopping. As she came around the corner by the tobacco counter, I stepped out. As I came out, the witch lady had to come out front. I walked up to her and said "There she is there's that witch lady."

Lisa looked and with her nicest voice to say said, "well Brenda that's my best friend." I was trying to recover from the embarrassment. When I said, "Well, she really isn't that bad." She stopped me and said "Brenda it's not nice to talk about anyone to someone else, because you never know who you might be saying it to. She isn't my friend but, she could have been."

I would never forget that lesson. It was then I took the time to get to know the lady I worked with. It turned out she was struggling to provide for her family. She would come and sit down in the evening, because she had been working three jobs. She was tired which made her cranky, and she was dealing with health issues.

As I began to show her compassion, she began to smile, and we became good friends. It was a few weeks later when I was standing in line to cash my check. I saw a friend of mine cashing her check. Now, she was having a hard time at the window, and the people in line were making fun of her. They were saying mean spirited names like; look she is so stupid she can't even sign her name, does she need to know how to place her X, why doesn't she get in back of the line, and she is holding everyone up. I got out

51

of line to see if I could help her. She was having a hard time getting her ID out of her purse. Yes, she was handicapped, but just needed a little help. So I helped her get what she needed, and then walked her out.

As I walked by them, they all hung their head. They never knew I was her friend, or they might not have said anything. Either way they needed to learn the lesson I did. There were some handicapped people in line that day, but it wasn't my friend. It was any and all of us, not willing to see the significance in others.

Thank you, God for your wonderful creation. We come in all shapes, colors, and designs, and yet your perfect love can abide in all of us.

"And above all these put on love, which binds everything together in perfect harmony" (Colossians 3:14, ESV).

God's Gift a Girl

I was married for three years, and I had just had my first child a girl named Michelle (which means Godly woman). We had just gotten home from the hospital, and I was sitting in the bedroom (so I'm guessing she was three or four days old). I went to the kitchen to get her a bottle, because it was about that time again. I had her in a swing with just a plastic band around her waist because that's the best they had back in the day. I was gone for only about three minutes, but when I came back Michelle was on the floor lying on a pillow that had been taken off of my bed. She wasn't crying, just lying there quietly. God made sure she was safe and placed on a pillow. She should have slid out the bottom, but if she did the plastic band would have wrapped around her neck. If she had fallen over the top she would have landed on her head, but no matter how she got there, she was lying on the pillow unharmed and resting. Wow, I started shaking and then tingling because God saw it fit to save her. I thank you Father, for protecting this young life. She must have something to do for the kingdom of God because she is still here.

"For I know the plans I have for you, declares the LORD, plans for peace and not for evil, to give you a future and a hope" (Jeremiah 29:11, ESV).

Being a new mother I didn't know much about taking care of a baby. I was told by the doctor, when I left the hospital that Michelle would eat about two ounces of formula every two hours. Since I am a literal person I kept her to that routine. This child cried and cried and cried and seemed as though she was never happy. My mother-in-law came over when she was about four weeks old and told me that she was hungry to feed her. Now, I wasn't going to listen to this woman, she didn't know anything about my baby. But she kept insisting that I give her a bottle, so I did. Michelle ate and went to sleep. When she left, I went back to the same routine of two-hour feedings. As I went to the doctors it was her six-week checkup. When they weighed her, she hadn't gained any weight. The doctor asked "how much is she eating?" I said "two ounces every two hours."

He told me that was my problem—I was starving her. He then asked if she was cranky and if she slept well? I told him, no way, she cries all the time and hardly sleeps, which makes my life miserable. He told me to take her home, let her eat as much as she wanted, and then we both would be better. I went home and she ate five ounces. She played, was happy, and even slept through the night.

Forgive me Father when you send people my way to help. I don't listen even if I don't know what to do. I sure wish I would be quick to listen. Even if it's not the one we want to hear from, it sure would save me a lot of grief. Pride stands in the way, even if wisdom is knocking at the door.

"Pride goes before destruction and a haughty spirit before a fall" (Proverbs 16:18, ESV).

Prayers Perfected

At this time I thought I was pregnant with my second child. All I could think about was having a boy, so I started praying for one. The moment I thought I might be pregnant all I wanted was a boy. This was an interesting time to say the least. I was pregnant. My husband had a problem with having one child. Even though it was three years later, a second child wasn't going to appeal to him much either. I went to the doctor's office and they examined me. The doctor performed quite a few tests since I was close to thirty years old. They told me I was four months along and sent me on my way.

I went to work that night trying to figure out how I was going to tell my husband that I was pregnant with our second child. Since I worked the night shift, and he worked an early shift I wouldn't see him until the weekend, which was two days away. I was working on the line when my supervisor called me over and said I had an important phone call. This was pretty weird since it was 10:45 p.m. I got to the phone and it was my doctor. He told me that I needed to come back to the office the next day to run some more tests.

It was scary because he said there was nothing conclusive, but he needed more tests. I went back to the doctor's office, they ran the tests, and then called me back in on Friday. When I got to the doctor's office he asked me to come into his private office. At that time, he told me that my baby had Down syndrome, and oh, by the way, it was a boy. He then said you have to decide what you are going to do with it? He said you are still able to have an abortion. We have to know soon because you are entering your fifth month, and we don't like doing them after that. I told him there was NO way I would have an abortion. I might not keep him, but I wouldn't have the abortion.

Now, to think I was having a BOY, but he wasn't healthy. So I went home. I could not go to work. I was too upset! Then God showed me my priorities were wrong. I quickly prayed, Father forgive me. I was so worried about the sex of the baby, and I never considered the health of the baby. As I got home my husband said what are you doing home? Without thinking I just said, I'm pregnant and it's a boy! And oh, by the way, he's has Down syndrome."

He said "what are you going to do?"

"I'm not going to get an abortion. I'm not special enough to raise a child with Down syndrome."

In my life I have known several families with Down syndrome kids, and they were amazing. However, they come with lots of health issues, and challenges with learning. It takes a lot of special care that I don't have. Then I went into my prayer closet and fell on my face before God and asked him to forgive me for being so narrow-minded. I told God that I wasn't so special that I could have a baby with Down syndrome.

As I continued to pray, I admitted to God that it took special people to raise these wonderful babies, and I just wasn't that special. I asked God to heal my child and make him perfectly healthy (at least in my eyes). I continued to pray every day. Four weeks went by, and I had to go back to the doctor's office to run some more tests to find out just how severe his Down syndrome was. The doctor told me he would call me back in a few days. When I came back from the doctor's office, they were waiting for me and called me back immediately. The doctor had a confused look on his face when he walked in. The doctor told me that he didn't know what happened, but the test results came back in, and your child is perfectly normal.

"I'm not sure what happened," the doc said, "But your child is as healthy as he can be with no trace of anything!

I said, "I know God healed him!"

I turned around and walked out with tears streaming down my face. Thank you Father for healing my child and giving me grace when my priorities weren't right!

"And if we know that He hears us, whatever we ask, we know that we have the requests which we have asked from him" (1 John 5:15 ESV).

Visits in the Night

When Michelle was 19 months old, she talked like a regular person, so it was nothing unusual to have a conversation with her and understand what she said. One particular evening I was putting her to bed, and she was sick, running a fever of 103. I gave her some medicine and laid her down.

She said "Momma, will you lie down with me?" I did, and after a few minutes I got up and prayed with her. She asked if I would hold her and sleep with her. I told her, "sweetie I can't, but you will be okay." She said "okay."

The next morning as I came in to check on her, she was sitting up playing and her fever was gone. I asked her if she slept okay last night. She said, "Yes, when you left JESUS came down and held me all night long." To think, I missed seeing Jesus, but I was so happy that He was there for her. Thank you Jesus for always showing up when I never knew I needed you. Michelle must have been sicker than I knew, and she needed your healing touch, but don't we all?

Visits in the Night Times Two

Michelle was about two and a half years old when she had a visit from Jesus again. It was evening, and we were getting ready to go to bed. I had prayed with her, and she said "Mom, don't go. I'm scared."

I said, "why sweetie, why are you scared?" She said, "I don't know, but I am." I said, "it will be okay, just lie down and talk to God and he will make you feel better."

I shut the door and went to bed. The next day I got up, and Michelle was lying down in her bed. I asked her, I guess you rested okay last night, right?

She said "Sure did! I prayed and Jesus came and stood over there in the corner all night, and I slept like a baby."

I smiled because I knew he had, because he cares so much for us. He is our Comforter and whatever it takes to remind us of that, he will do. I thank you Jesus, for filling in where I left off.

"If you remain in Me, and My Words remain in you, whatever you desire you will ask, and it shall happen to you" (John 15:7, ESV).

Miracles Making Michael

When I was six months pregnant with my son, I had just gotten out of the doctor's office and my husband said, "Let's go get a bite to eat." I wasn't eating much; in fact I had already lost twenty-five pounds since I got pregnant. So we went to a steak house since I was low on iron, I figured I better eat some protein. The first bite I took had a strange taste to it, but I took another bite and said, "I'm not sure, but I think there is something wrong with the steak or mushrooms. Either way, I don't want to eat anymore". We went home. Later that evening I started getting very sick, violently sick. By the end of the night there was nothing left in my stomach and I was so dehydrated that I had red spots all over. We had to go to the hospital. When I got there, they weighed me and I had lost ten pounds in one night. I ended up staying for three days because they were worried about the baby. Again God was taking care of us both; seeing us through any trials we might have. Thank you again, Father for giving me a healthy baby!

It was six weeks later and I was seven and a half months along when I started having back pains. I thought, *NO way I cannot be going into labor.* We went to the hospital and found out that I was passing kidney stones. This was worse than the labor pains and I had gone through that three other times in my life. Now this was causing me to go into premature labor. They gave me some meds that would help with the pain and get me through the difficult time. After three more days, I was released and had somehow passed the stone.

You have to wonder what is going on, having gone through three different ordeals before this baby was even born. Every six weeks from four and a half months someone/something was trying to harm this baby. Thank you Jesus for giving me a healthy baby, no matter the cost. It is always worth what we have to go through to see God's perfect plan.

When my son was born, we named him Michael (his name means Godly Man). They say give them a name and it will become that. Guess what happened next and when? He was six weeks old and we were in a grocery store. I had Michael in a car seat, sitting on a grocery cart. I turned to grab Michelle's hand and when I did the car seat just flipped over onto the cement floor. Michael's face hit the ground, and he let out the biggest scream that no mother wants to hear. My husband came around the corner and grabbed him up and headed straight for the hospital. When we got there, they found nothing wrong, other than a knot on his forehead.

Amazing that he continued to live through everything while I was pregnant, and now that he was born he falls head first four feet onto solid concrete and nothing is wrong? Once again, when we pray God honors our prayers. Michael continues to be healthy and nothing seems to faze him, or maybe we can just say God's hedge of protection is around him. Thank you Father for showing me through this whole thing that your Word is true. My baby is healthy. Now may I be the kind of parent that treasures such a miracle from God.

Images I Want to Forget

As kids we love doing things that are daring, and exciting. Kids have no fear because they are young. As an adult, wisdom and age are on your side. There is no way you would even think of riding, doing, or attempting anything scary. I hate scary movies. I don't like the images they leave. People tell me its entertainment, but I don't see it that way. My mom went to see Jaws when I was a kid, and when she came home she told me I could never see that movie.

To this day I never have, I trusted her guidance. However, I loved going to haunted houses. I think it was because they startle you. I love to jump out of places and scare people. It's fun to watch their reaction. I decided I want to go to a haunted house at this particular time. My husband is holding Michelle who was around two and a half years old. As a responsible parent, I should have left her home; I didn't. I entered the scary zone! As Michelle began to walk behind me, she was the only one with common sense and quickly grabbed her dad and said "pick me up."

She hides her head in his chest and all she has done is hear the music. It's me winding through the maze. All of a sudden there is a HUGE chainsaw about an inch away from my face. It was a real chainsaw and running. This chainsaw startles me so bad I soiled myself. Go ahead, laugh, I can now. I look at my husband and said, "Guess we have to get out of here." He asked "why?"

I tell him, and he just shook his head. We rushed through the rest of the attraction, and it was very startling all the way through. As we got to the end, this punk that had made me soil myself was waiting on me. As I came around the corner thinking the attraction was over, he comes running after me with that sorry chainsaw!

Once again, as if I had anything left, I ran and soiled myself at the same time. Now, I have to figure how I'm going to sit in the car without having this all over the seats. I take some diapers from Michael. Who would have thought at age twenty-nine, I would need diapers, but I did. Now ask yourself, why in the world I would go to a haunted house when I won't even watch a scary movie. God didn't want me to do either. I threw my money away; I embarrassed myself. I left an impression on my young daughter. Most important I was disobedient to what God wanted for my life. God never wants us to have images of anything but him. Thank you, Father that you want to protect us from things that will do us harm, in more ways the one.

It's Jesus's Birthday

It was Christmas time, and we all were going Christmas caroling to all the older people in our church. We were driving from one house to another. Michelle age three, started talking to me about Christmas. She said Mom, "its Jesus's birthday, right?"

I said, "Right." Then she said, "I want to give him a present."

I said, "Sure."

All twenty-five of us mostly teenagers, four adults, and, of course, Michelle got out of the bus. When we were done, we all got back in and headed toward our next place. One of the youth probably about thirteen decided to talk to Michelle.

She said "Michelle, it's Jesus's birthday, right?

Michelle said "Right.

You're going to give him a present right?"

Michelle said, "Right."

Then she said "How are you going to give it to him?"

Without missing a beat Michelle said "Ahh...when he comes back to get me."

I was surprised by her response, but I don't know why. She probably knew better than all of us. Thank you, God, for her childlike faith that never questions what you say. Wouldn't we all do better if we just believed because God said it? "And they fell down and worshipped him. Then, opening their treasures, they offered him gifts, gold, and frankincense, and myrrh" (Matthew 2:11, ESV).

God Will Use Anyone

I was asked to teach a Sunday school class for four-year-olds. Teaching the class was easy, and having my daughter Michelle as one of my students made it enjoyable. The class had about forty-two enrolled. Only six or seven attended on a regular basis. Coming into the class, I knew I needed to get the kids excited about Sunday school again. I got on the phone and started calling everyone and invited them to Sunday school and to church. We were very pleased by the fourth or fifth week we had about thirty kids.

When I got to the class, I wanted to do more than just to teach them Bible stories. I told them we were going to learn to memorize Bible verses. If they learned all the memory verses, I would throw them a party, and give them all Jesus's shirts at the end of the year. The kids were very excited about winning T-shirts and having a party. They took to it like duck to water. The kids would come in the class every Sunday and tell me their memory verses before they did anything else. There was one little girl, whose name was Sylvia who didn't come very regularly, she would come one week and miss two.

Surprisingly as soon as she got there, she would ask me for the verses. She then would go into the corner of the room and start memorizing them. I was so pleased because at one point we had forty-one of the forty-two kid's enrolled who showed up for class of which, thirty five attended regularly and thirty one kids memorized all of the memory verses. The end of the year finally came around, and I told the kids that we were going to say all the memory verses together the next week. Please come and be prepared to say all of them I said.

By the time the next week came, all the kids were there, and they were awesome! They said one verse after another, and right then the pastor walked by. He popped his head around the corner and heard the thirty-five kids in unison saying all the memory verses. The pastor asked me what was going on. I simply told him that I wanted to teach them more than just Bible stories; I wanted to teach them memory verses. The pastor was impressed that we had learned over forty verses in one year.

He said, "Wow! Amazing! How old are they?"

I said, "Only four years old?"

He asked to show the congregation what the kids have learned.

I said, "Sure."

"How about it kids, do you want to show the church what we have learned?"

They all screamed, "Yeah!"

The next week about six to ten people came by the classroom and asked if we would able to get in front of the church so quickly. Most people have to wait six months and still don't get to share anything. I simply told them the kids were excited about the opportunity to show the church what they had learned.

That morning we practiced our memory verses. The kids had a Bible story, and got in a circle to pray. I asked the kids what they wanted to pray for. Sylvia was the first to raise her hand. She said, "I want my mom and dad to come and see me next week perform during church." The next kid also said they wanted Sylvia's mom and dad to come too. Every child in the circle wanted the same thing, in fact all thirty-six kids asked for Sylvia's mom and dad to come to church.

So we prayed in unison, all for that one request. Prayer time was incredible. When I got ready to leave, Sylvia's grandmother was standing in the doorway. She told me that she heard everyone in the class praying for Sylvia's mom and dad. They aren't going to come. Grandma said that, "if it weren't for me, Sylvia wouldn't have gotten to come as much as she did."

She said "I would go over to Sylvia's house every Sunday, knock on the door. If Sylvia's parents answered, I would go in and get her ready. I might have to give her a bath, dress her, and then feed her.

The times she wasn't here, her parents had just refused to get up. It has been a struggle all year just to get her here." Then she looked at me and said "so don't expect for them to come." I told her that is what Sylvia wanted to pray for, so we did.

The next week came, and the kids were so excited. I got to buy thirty-one T-shirts, and they all put them on and wore them out in front of the congregation. We all lined up preparing to go into sanctuary. To help calm them, I told them to keep looking at me. There were over three thousand five hundred people in the Sanctuary. As they all got situated and ready to recite ten scriptures, the pastor asked me to come on stage.

The pastor told me to tell the congregation what I was doing. I told them that this year we had learned over forty-one memory verses in our Sunday school class. I would like to show you a little sample of what we learned. The kids sang out in unison; greater is he that lives in me than he that lives in the world (1 John 4:4), I can do all things through Christ that strengthens me (Philippians 4:13), and eight more verses.

The kids were incredible, and the crowd gave them a standing ovation. I thought we were done but the pastor called me back up there again.

He said "tell us Ms. Brenda, what made you do this."

I said, "I wanted to teach them more than just Bible stories. While it has been a pleasure to have these kids in my class, I have learned more from them than they have ever learned from me. I know that we all say that learning scriptures is hard but if these four-year-olds can do it so can you."

Pastor said, "Can you show us a little more?"

I said, "Sure."

Just as I was walking down from the stage Sylvia grabbed my skirt and yanks it. She said "look Mrs. Brenda" as she is pointing and tears running down her face.

"It's my mom and dad, they came!"

I said, "Oh my goodness, that's so cool. Now do a good job so they can see you." The kids said ten more verses without missing a beat and got another standing ovation. I then told the kids that they could all go sit with their parents. Sylvia was stilling crying as she went to sit with her mom and dad. All the kids were excited, because they were going to have the party after church. The pastor preached his message, and then he gave the salvation invitation. Michelle grabbed my skirt and yanked on it, then said, "Look mom, look."

I said, "Michelle honey, bow your head."

She yanked again and I said, "What?"

She said, "Look down there. It was Sylvia's mom and dad."

Tears started streaming down my cheeks as I saw them walking down the aisle. The Pastor stopped the service and said folks; you just have to hear what I just heard. Sylvia's dad held the microphone, and told us in a very trembling voice, "You see, I just wanted to tell you that I'm here today because of my daughter. She would come home every week and say those crazy verses over and over. Sylvia would beg me, to help with her memory verses."

She would say "Daddy please, please help me, I just got to learn my verses. So I can get a T-shirt, and go to the party."

"At first I just ignored Sylvia. As her dad I couldn't be bothered with Sylvia or those verses. When Sylvia first started with these memory verses, my wife and I were doing drugs, drinking, and smoking. After about three months, my wife and I walked away from drugs. Sylvia was persistent with saying those stupid verses over and over. Then three or four months went by, me and my wife and without thinking about it, we had quit drinking. It was then I started helping her with her verses every week.

"Sylvia and I would go over them together, and I cherished those times. I can tell you today that we don't even smoke anymore. God's Word is powerful and it changes lives. I'm here today accepting Jesus as my savior, because my daughter loved me enough to share the Word of God with me. God will use anyone, even a four-year-old if that's what it takes to get your attention."

With tears in his eyes he reached down and picked up Sylvia, and hugged her and his wife. They say a child will lead them, but in Sylvia's family, her dad leads them now. God will use anyone!

"I thank you, Father, Lord of heaven and earth, that you have hidden these things from the wise and understanding and revealed them to little children; yes, Father, for such was your gracious will" (Luke 10:21, ESV).

Sock it to me

When Michael was three years old, he was completely honest about everything. He didn't know what lying was about. As a child, he had rules. One rule he was told was that he could not go outside without an adult. He could go in the backyard but only if he asked. This particular day he decided that for whatever reason, he was going to go outside. Michael went in the front yard without telling anyone. When I heard the front door slam, I looked out the front window. Michael had gone next door, grabbed a tricycle, and started riding it in the street. Then Michael ran across the road. He knocked on the neighbor's door to get a friend to play with him. He proceeded to come back across the street. As Michael came back to the front door, I hurried and locked the door. I wanted to teach him a lesson. He and his friend came across the street and then rang the doorbell. When I didn't open the door, Michael started knocking. I guess he wasn't scared because he knew I would open it sooner or later.

When I opened the door, he said, "Can me and Jeremy play?"

I told Jeremy he would have to go home, Michael was in big trouble, and he couldn't play right then. I grabbed Michael by the arm, and told him to go to his bedroom. He needed to think about what he had done. I gave him about thirty minutes. I was thinking that he would be in tears by now, because he was wondering what was going to happen to him. As I came into the room, Michael was just playing with his toys. I told him, first of all mister you are in BIG trouble. Tell me what you did wrong, you're getting a spanking. This was something I did with my kids as they were growing up. I asked them what they did wrong, so they would not just guess why they were getting punished. Sometimes, as a child, when I was growing up, we got spankings, and we never knew what they were for. Michael told me, "Well, first I went outside without asking. Then I went over to the neighbor's house, and got a toy, and played with it in the street. Then I just left it in the street without putting it back. Then I crossed the street without looking. Then I went to my friend's house without asking, and asked him to play without asking you. Then I crossed back across the street without looking again."

I told him, "I guess you understand why you are getting a spanking then?"

He looked at me and said, "And…I wore my new socks outside. As he lifted up his foot he said, I got holes in them."

Well, now that was something I didn't know or I wouldn't have known. He was already in trouble, so he wanted me to know everything. At that point I was blown away at his honesty, so I gave him a swat on the backside.

I said, "Don't do that ever again."

He looked at me with complete trust and said, "I won't."

Can you tell how wonderful it is to know that when someone tells you something you can take it to the bank and write a check because that's their word? God is that way with us. We can take his Word, trust it, take it to heart, and live it out because he will never break any of his promises to us. Thank you God that we can have that childlike faith to trust you with everything in our lives because your word is true and you cannot lie!

"In hope of eternal life, which God, that cannot lie, promised before the world began" (Titus 1:2, ESV).

I Have Jesus

It was Thanksgiving, and Michelle was in the first grade. The class was asked to bring something for their Thanksgiving feast: chips, cookies, pop, and candy—a true feast for kids. Michelle went to school, and came home saying she had fun.

I said "really? Tell me about it." So she did. She told me they all sat down in a circle, and had their feast; her favorite were the cookies. The teacher went around the circle asking all the kids what they were the most thankful for. One kid said his cat, another his dog, one said his bike, another said her house, one said her friends, and another said her family.

Michelle was the last one they came to, she looked at her and said Michelle what are you the most thankful for?

Michelle said, "I'm thankful I have Jesus living in my heart."

The teacher said, "No Michelle, you don't get it."

Then all the kids laughed. I asked Michelle "how did that made you feel sweetie, when everyone laughed at you. Did that make you mad?"

She said, "No momma it made me sad. If they had Jesus living in their hearts they wouldn't have laughed."

She walked away with the knowledge that they don't have anything without Jesus!

Easter Kid Style

We were gearing up for Easter; it's one of the kids' favorite holidays. They make Easter even more fun, because they see it so much BIGGER. I was sitting down in the living room, and started talking to Michael. I asked him why we celebrate Easter.

He said "because Jesus came back alive."

I said, "so what about the Easter bunny."

He said, "I got that figured out too. You see the Easter bunny is just a man in a costume. He is so happy Jesus came back alive; he goes around and gives candy to the little children."

I smiled because that made sense. To think a child can explain something no one else could. Thank you Father for being the reason we celebrate every day!

"But the angel said to the women, "Do not be afraid, for I know that you seek Jesus who was crucified. He is not here, for he has risen, as he said. Come; see the place where he lay" (Matthew 28:5–6 ESV).

This Message Is for YOU

We were in church one Sunday morning, and it was services as usual. All of a sudden, right in the middle of the preaching, he stopped. The pastor announced there is someone here that will not make it home.

Out of nowhere the pastor said, "You need to accept Jesus as your Savior today."

Then he went on preaching, and stopped and said again, "Today is your day. I implore you to accept Jesus before it's too late."

The spirit was heavy in the place by now. Everyone could feel something happening, and then the pastor stopped again to say, "Today is your day of salvation. Do not put it off, because when you leave here it will be the last time anyone ever sees you." He then stopped preaching and gave an invitation.

There were at least fifty people that came forward and made decisions. I'm sure there were more, but only those people went forward. After the service it was pretty quiet, because we had just witnessed God showing mercy to someone. We got on the road and were heading to lunch. When we got on the ramp to the highway there was a car to the right that had been completely destroyed. They said the driver didn't make it. Ask the question if you like, but I don't know if he accepted Jesus as his savior. I pray he was one of those that came down, but only God knows. We thank you Father that we can know for sure where we will be when we die.

"Behold now is the favorable time; behold, now is the day of salvation" (2 Corinthians 6:2, ESV).

Just for Fun

Michelle was six years old, and she wanted to play basketball. She joined a team, and she learned a lot during her first year. She enjoyed it so much that she wanted to do it again a second year. However, when we contacted the coach the next year he told us, he wasn't even going to coach a team, so I decided to coach a team.

I contacted everyone from the year before, and half of them said they were going to play for the old coach. The other half didn't get picked up, so I picked them up. I picked up every player that nobody wanted, and decided that they should make a team. Our team was called *Just for Fun*. I started by telling all the girls that I wanted them to learn to play together. No one player was more important than the other. As a team we could win!

As the story goes, the girls practiced hard and played for fun. After the first six games, of which they had won all, they came up against the coach that didn't want six of the girls. We shook hands, and I smiled at him. He seemed a little embarrassed that I found out his secret.

As a coach I got to know each and every one of the girl's weaknesses, and strengths. I played them according to what the team needed. It was during the fourth quarter, and it had come down to us being ahead by four points. All I wanted to do is to run off the clock. I gave it to our *ball hog* and told her just to dribble it out for two and half minutes; which she did beautifully.

Then Michelle took the ball and scored; we won! The coach didn't even shake my hand. The girls just smiled. They knew they played well, had fun, and learned. Here's an interesting point for you to know. The girls won all fourteen games that year. Then the girls went into the playoffs and had to play the old coach's team again for the finals. He ended up getting kicked out of the game for his unsportsmanlike conduct. The girls won by fifteen points, and took home the trophy. Which was cool, but not as cool as seeing the value in people that others can't or won't. Isn't it awesome that God sees the value in us and works with us? Teaches us and is proud of us when things come together and work for his purpose.

We Did It

Michael decided that he wanted to play basketball as well, which made it the youngest team in the league. While the rest of the kids were two years older than them, their team still enjoyed every moment. They started out just being able to dribble the ball effectively down the court, and got excited when they did it. Next was not double-dribbling, and then not fouling every time someone shot.

After the first game, we realized we were in the same league, but only lost by twenty-two points. Every game brought new accomplishments, and they never quit despite the fact that even after four games they hadn't even gotten the basketball close to the rim. Thirteen games came and went and the season was over.

They hadn't even scored one point, but it didn't matter. The ball had at least touched the rim a couple of times, when they shot it. The team celebrated every victory. They either weren't getting beat by as much, or they stole the ball, blocked a shot, and even tie up the ball. They had the right attitude the entire season, and I was just happy that we taught them some skills along the way.

The best game was the last one of the season. The boys managed to get the toughest team in the league; the other team was talking about how we were going down well, at least our points. The game went as usual until the fourth quarter when I happened to mention to their coach and referees that we didn't care if we lost; but we would just like to score at least one basket.

With about forty-six seconds left to go in the game, the referees stopped the clock and kept telling our boys to take a shot. Every time the other team touched the ball they called a foul, and they gave it back to our boys. The coach from the other team caught onto what they were doing, and he told his boys to lower their hands.

The other coach then called over his boys, and told them to pass our boys the ball and let them shoot. So every time the other team rebounded, they would pass it off to one of our boys, and tell them to shoot. Our boys were a little confused, because no matter what they did they got the ball and got to shoot. This went on for three minutes. Then the crowd finally figured out what everyone was trying to do, so they started yelling "shoot the ball, shoot the ball, you can do it, you can do it."

In unison it went from our fans to their fans. Everyone in the building at this time had stepped in to witness what was going on, and cheering our boys on. There were probably about two hundred people yelling and rooting for our boys to make a basket. After about twenty shots at the basket, it finally happened. One of the boys threw the ball up at the basket, and it went in. The whole place exploded! You would have thought we had won the championship. Wow, to think we just got our very first basket! Everyone was giving our boys high fives and patting them on the back. That was the best moment of the season. Everyone came together for the greater cause—seeing others reaching a goal.

Thank you God for letting them see they were winners all year long. They never saw the score as important because it didn't change who they were becoming! "I have fought the good fight, I have finished the race, I have kept the faith" (2 Timothy 4:7, ESV).

Thou Shall Not Steal

I was just recently married, and I needed to find a job. There were numerous things I did previously. I had worked at a grocery store, gas station, oil company, US office, tag agency, tobacco store, produce manager, Chuck wagon, and SPD-instrument tech, which I had just lost. They let me go. I wanted to get married, and they needed me at work. I applied for a job at the airport.

I quickly moved from position to position, until I had worked at every position within the company. I knew all the ins and outs of the company. I got to manage one area, and even worked into the morning position. I know it wasn't good for me, because I was quickly taking things, stealing.

Everyone I knew was taking things; it was too easy. They had so much overhead that they had a hard time keeping up with what was coming in, and what was going out. I had lots of opportunity to make extra cash and I did. I told my husband that I was making good tips, and so we bought a car and eventually bought a house. I got all of this while at the job, but eventually I started feeling guilty. I asked God to help me stop the stealing. I was sincere in my asking, but when I went back to work I continued to steal. One day, at church, I went to the altar, and asked God to make a way for me not to take anything.

The next day at work no one would give me a break, so after seven hours I called the manager. When the manager came to give me a break, I said to him, handle it, and walked off. They later said because I left the premises, I resigned so I no longer had a job.

Thank you God for helping me find a way out. It might not have been exactly what I had expected, but it got me out of there. Two days later I landed a job working in the same type of environment. What are you doing God? Putting me in this same situation? A convenience store where I could take anything I wanted, but I refused to give into temptation. One night I was sweeping up the floor, and happened to grab a two-cent piece of gum and started chewing. I panicked because I remembered I hadn't paid for it.

I quickly ran to my car picked up the mats, and pushed my hand in the seats looking for anything. After ten minutes, I finally found two pennies. I knew I didn't have any money, because I got to work on fumes. I didn't even know how I was going to get home. I was not worried about that. I was just concerned with getting to work. I paid the money for the gum, walked outside, and started sweeping the parking lot. I got to the doorway and picked up the mat, and as I picked it up there was $20 lying right there.

WOW, to think I was faithful in paying for the gum, and God rewarded me two thousand times what I paid. I now had the money to pay for gas to get home—three times blessed. Just two weeks later, I got a good job that paid twice as much as I was making, and I stayed there for ten years.

Thank you, God, for teaching me a valuable lesson—that as we do the right thing no matter what, we receive blessings beyond measure. No one would have missed that gum, but then God isn't anyone, He is the only one. God sees it all and is a rewarder of those who diligently seek him.

Oh, by the way, I lost everything I got with that money, the house, car, and more. God wouldn't allow me to keep anything—I got dishonestly. I ended up living in a house where the mice outnumbered the roaches, and, by the way, I hate both. We were in a neighborhood where they had shootings every week. One time a helicopter even flew over our house, and used a microphone to tell us to go inside the house.

They were chasing a criminal. I hated that house because the mice would come out, and taunt me during the day. The roaches were so bad they didn't care if it was day or night. I told my kids that they had to keep their shoes on. The mice would eat their toes off, mostly it was my phobia. The kids believed me so much, that they wore shoes to bed…I have to say, so did I.

Also I had purchased a new car, and lost it because my driving was so bad that the insurance was more than the car payment. I lost my license for one year and I had to be driven everywhere I needed to go. When I did get a car, it was pieced together. No kidding; it was a station wagon that was mostly yellow with red doors and a blue tailgate. Now here is where I got taught a huge lesson.

God is not going to take you anywhere unless you are grateful for where you are already. So, while it took me a year to finally be thankful for where we were. God showed me that all the stuff we have is nothing compared to our integrity. So while we owned absolutely nothing, I was never more content because God was pleased with whom I was becoming. Thank you, God, for being patient while I took so long to learn!

"The thief comes only to steal and kill and destroy. I came that they may have life and have it abundantly" (John 10:10, esv).

Speak to Me

One day while I was going to work, it was early and I was running late. They couldn't open the store unless I was there. I was the only one with keys. It was 5:15 a.m., and I was supposed to open up at 5:00 a.m. My radio was messing up, and I was jiggling the wires trying to get it to work. Then I began hitting the top of the radio, thinking I could get it to work.

I turned the corner, and was almost at work when a policeman stopped me. Goodness! If that isn't all I needed! He told me that I was speeding. I had run a red light, and I had been swerving all over the road. I told him I was messing with my radio, and was late for work.

He asked "can I see your driver's license;" I looked at him and said "NO, my sister has my driver's license. She went bar hopping last night."

He then asked, "Can I see your insurance card?"

I said, "No I have no insurance. I have had too many tickets, so I can't afford any insurance. Can you please give me the ticket so I can just get to work?"

He proceeded to lecture me for the next thirty minutes on the dangers of driving while not paying attention, speeding, and running red lights. I was so frustrated, because every minute he spoke it meant I could not be at work. I would have rather gotten the tickets than hear all that he had to say. He let me go, and he didn't give me anything, not even a warning. To think God wants us to slow down, and listen to him, so that we don't get into trouble, but we are too busy to listen. Thank you, God, that you continue to speak to me even when I give you attitude—you never stop drawing me back.

"My sheep hear my voice, and I know them, and they follow me" (John 10:27, ESV).

To Be Used by YOU

I was helping the youth out at church. We decided to have a lock-in with all the kids from second grade to fifth grade. The theme was Glamour Shots, God Sees Us as Beautiful. We had several stations the kids could come to: nails, hair, clothes, make-up, and accessories. We had boys and girls alike, all ready to pose for the camera. Three hundred kids showed up, and we only had three other adults to help me out.

I wasn't expecting so many kids, but it wouldn't have changed anything about it. We had twenty-five pizzas, twenty bags of cookies, forty three-liter sodas, twenty-eight bags of chips, and some games. Then we got everyone together to share a story. It ended up being the first time I gave my testimony in front of a group of people.

I gave an invitation, which I never knew was going to happen. The kids were very attentive, and once the invitation was given around thirty kids came up, and accepted Jesus into their lives.

To my shock Michelle was one of them. I was so excited, but I sent her to someone else. I wanted to make sure she knew the decision she had just made. So Michelle prayed and accepted Jesus into her life.

Thank you, God, for drawing all these children to you, for sending your son to die for them, let them live for you. To think they are so young, but never too young to be used by you.

"And this is the testimony that God gave us eternal life, and this life is in his Son" (1 John 5:11 ESV).

Remembering the Ride

A group of us got together and decided we wanted to take our kids on a trip to Florida—Walt Disney World to be exact. Now being the resourceful ones, we had four adults and four kids so this was going to take a lot of money. So we put our heads together and came up with a plan. I worked for a company that rewarded us in McDonald's coupons. I worked for a meat company that would give you a $5 coupon every time you found a foreign object in the meat. It could be anything from a plastic glove, to bullets, and even knifes, because some people dropped knifes accidentally in the meat. I must have gotten about two to three a week. I already had $50 in coupons when we talked. Then we thought we could save money by sharing one hotel room.

Yeah kids on the floor on blow up mattresses. The girls shared a bed, and the boys shared one. Then we decided we would rent a minivan for the week, which we could all pile into, and I mean pile. Then we found out that if you buy your ticket in advance from the Disney store in the mall you could save forty percent, which was a HUGE, savings. So by taking one vehicle instead of two we saved $400 in gas. We also brought an ice chest full of sandwich fixings, drinks, chips, and cookies. We figured doing all of this would allow us to take our kids to something we had never got to experience. The total cost should have been about $5,600.00, but by the time we squeezed our nickels and dimes it cost us $1,922.00. Now here is where the adventure begins.

We had to pack a minivan with eight people's clothes, and food for the week. We took out the front two bench seats and that opened up the area for the kids to sit and play games. The guys did all the driving on the trip, while the girls watched the kids. The luggage was stacked to the roof in the back, and the ice chests, yes, that's right—two were put in the backbench. The kids were as happy as could be—seat belts were not enforced so they were playing in the middle of the floor. We hit the road from Oklahoma City to Kissimmee, Florida. Everything was great until we had to stop quickly then the luggage fell forward on us, and the kids. So we stopped stacked and started again.

Now I wish I could tell you we fixed the problem, but that was not the case. This must have happened about ten times in a twenty-one hour trip. The kids were grabbing their heads every time the guys would be putting on their brakes. Not every time the brakes hit they all came down. All of this just added to our adventure—not the kids but ours. When we got there we checked into the room, and got everything set up.

We got to go to Epcot center, Walt Disney world, Universal studios, and more. We must have rode every ride, and sometimes twice depending if it cooled you off. There was one time we were watching a log ride come down the last drop before we figured it out, we all got the BEST splash of our lives. Talk about cooled off and more than we wanted. Needless to say it was an adventure. It was nonstop walking, riding, and shows. If everyone was scared to ride the ride, they would dare me. I don't back down on a dare, so I ended up riding them all. Between you and me, I would never do it now.

There was one ride that took you up about twenty-five stories and dropped you. I just thought it was taking you up and showing you the sights and then bringing you back down. It was sort of like a bungee drop. If I had known, I would have never, and I repeat never, gotten on that silly ride. It was after this ride that I lost my nerve for every other ride in my life. It was like it showed me I could get hurt, and I wasn't about to do that.

Weird how one ride can change your opinion, but it did. I never rode a roller coaster again, or anything that took you up over two stories. I guess I hated the feeling of feeling hopeless. Forget that it was supposed to be fun; I wanted my feet firmly planted on the ground. The kids enjoyed everything, and got to experience things they had never seen before and loved every minute.

The kids never complained until we started coming back. They we're sick of sandwiches, sick of chips, cookies, and believe this or not sick of McDonald's. We had over $300 in coupons, and we ate there for breakfast and dinner. We would be at the park during the day, so we would splurge, and treat ourselves there. On the way back, the boys decided they didn't like packing the luggage every thirty minutes, so they got bungee cords and really tied it down. We only had three spills all the way back. As we look back, it was so much fun, and we loved being able to take a vacation together. It was the last time we all got together as a group, so we truly cherished the time.

Thank you, God, for making a way for us to go and for planting my feet on solid ground. Thank you, God, that I am never hopeless because you're in control.

Speak Life

Speak words of encouragement whenever you can. I did and here is what happened. I was working at a meat processing plant. I was checking the line when my friend Steve came by. He seemed a little upset, so I asked him if there was anything wrong. He politely told me it doesn't matter, and kept walking. A few minutes later he stopped to talk for a minute, and as he talked there was more to it.

He was so upset he had tears rolling down his face. He had an argument with his stepson, and got so angry that they got into a fight. He had an argument with his wife who just happened to work where we did as well. I told him that he was such a compassionate, kind, and thoughtful person that everyone that knew him liked him. I also told him that he was so talented and God wanted to use him in a special way. We talked a little longer, and I felt like he was better.

Later after work his wife talked to me. She said that they were doing badly. She asked if I could come by to talk to him. I said sure I would be happy to. So I went to their house after work, sat down in the living room, and listened as he talked. I was kind of wondering what I could say to help this situation. As we sat and talked, all I could come up with is that God loved him and had a better plan for his life.

He told me about all the fighting, and how he felt so bad. All I knew was that he needed someone that would listen, and not judge. When we were through it was four hours later. I left him with a prayer that he could pray if he wanted to change his life. I reminded him that God loves him, and truly wants to make a difference in his life. The next day he came up to me at work, and was smiling. He told me he got before God and asked him to forgive him, and come into his life. Wow! He accepted Jesus! God was changing him before my eyes. Not to mention his wife was overjoyed at the difference in just one night. I don't know what happened, but I do know God can do anything with a broken heart.

Later he told me he had been getting ready to end it. Before I came to talk to him, he was going to drive himself off a bridge and kill himself.

Thank you, God for Your perfect timing. He didn't feel he had any other way out, but you gave him hope and helped him make a better choice. Thank you, Father, for letting me speak words of life into this young man's life. Isn't it cool that your words not only change lives but change destinies. I was privileged to see him get baptized a few weeks later, and his whole family was there to celebrate his new walk and what a new walk it was.

"Follow me, and I will make you fishers of men" (Matthew 4:19, esv).

Faithful Friends

The Bible talks about a friend that sticks closer than a brother. It was about this time that I was going through a lot of difficult personal issues—one of them was a divorce. While at work it was business as usual except for people talking. Since we all worked together…the rumors were really flying.

However this one lady, Margie, didn't listen to the rumors; she didn't have time for it. Every day at work the people that I was working with made it extremely hard on me, and I seemed to always be behind. Margie would come up once every thirty minutes, and get me caught up. Now she never knew what a blessing she was to me, but she definitely was a bright spot in my day.

One day I noticed she was a little upset. I asked her if there was anything wrong, she told me, "I'm all right and walked away. Then as we were in the storage room getting supplies we got to talk a little more. Every day we would open up, and talk more. We would find ourselves hurrying up to get things done, so we could go talk, and have some down time. One day she opened up, and told me she was going through a divorce. She also shared her living arrangements. I told her she could come, and stay with me since the kids were still with their dad. She said you don't know me from nobody, and you would offer your house to us?

I said, "Sure, you need a place to stay I have a place, and I would love to have you."

That was the start of a true friendship, one that has stood the test of time. She has always been there for me, and I for her. We might not see each other for a few weeks or even months, but we always pick up where we left off. After my divorce, I shared joint custody of the kids. I took Michelle with me, and moved to Texas. When Margie's divorce was final, she moved to Texas as well. Now that's when you know you have a friend willing to leave everything to be close to the ones that stick closer than a brother; or in this case a sister!

We had three things in common, we both loved God, we both needed a friend, and we both loved being around each other. God knew we needed each other, and so he forged a friendship that would stand the test of time. Thank you God for always providing for both of us in ways we never knew we needed.

Love Never Fails

While at work my friend Daniel and I had just checked the production lines. He came running around the corner and asked me to watch his lines he had to leave. Then out of nowhere they tell us all to turn off the lines and come to the conference room. As we came in and sat down we began listening to the TV. A report about someone bombing the Federal building downtown came on. We were all shocked and speechless at what we were seeing. Next one of the managers told us that if we had anyone that was working in the federal building, we probably needed to go to the police station and check on them. Daniel's wife was one of the ladies working in the building, that's why he took off.

She was the last person they got out of the building after they imploded it. Then another co-worker, Matthew, had a nephew in the daycare at the bombing site. He didn't make it and he was only four years old. As the reports came out, the more we found out about friends and family. My friend Cathy was working at the police department when it happened. She ran over to the sight; she said it was literally raining blood. They saw a man in the window of the building where rescue was trying to get to them. When they did reach him he was only half there. It was a very horrific time for everyone in Oklahoma at the time. Cathy was responsible for taking all the fingerprints of all the bodies that came out of the building. Her hair was brown when she started out, but six weeks later the front half was solid white. I had several people coming by my house because they couldn't stand to be at their house. Everyone was sitting around just listening to all the bad reports from the bombing.

The TV station played nonstop news for the first month, and then after that they allow regular TV on some stations. It was just terrible, and no one was healing from it. I was grateful I had people coming over. At least, we could talk, pray for families and healing. As stories unfolded though, we heard incredible stories. For instance, as one man was taking photos of the building he got the clouds in the air. When he got the photo developed there were several angels you could see in the cloud.

One guy said he was on his way to the building that morning, when he got a flat, so he didn't make it to work on time. Another lady told us that she had an appointment there but she locked her keys in the car. Then when she finally got them out she still had time to make it, but spilled coffee on herself, so she had to go change. Another man was walking up to the building, and realized he forgot the briefcase in the car, so he walked back. It saved his life. Daniel's wife had just started working there, and she didn't have time to enroll their son in the daycare, or he would have been there.

There were hundreds of stories of people that should have been there but for whatever reason didn't make it. There was a great revival in the city, people were going to church. We had so many people reaching out to help their neighbors there was a tremendous outpouring of kindness toward one another.

Thank you, God, that when people go through something so life altering. They turn to the only hope they have…YOU! Thank you, God for healing people and bringing them to a place where you could rebuild.

Steer Clear

Michelle was having some friends over to the house, and before I knew it, she was gone. No Big deal, until I answered the phone, and hear on the other end Michelle screaming "help me MOM, help me."

I said, "Where are you at? What is wrong?"

No one ever wants to hear your child screaming, and crying in the phone. Come to find out Michelle had jumped into a golf cart, and headed down the hill with one of her girlfriends. The only problem is that we live on a very steep incline, and it was about a football field long. As I went down to the corner, I could see the golf cart turned on its side and Michelle was lying on the side of the ditch. Evidently, the brakes went out, and the girl driving the cart jumped out. Michelle was on the passenger side trying to steer it safely down the hill, but the cart had other things in mind. As it came to the bottom of the hill, she tried to turn it around the corner, that's when it flipped. A witness said she was thrown out of the cart, and slid fifty feet or so.

All the while the cart was rolling on top of her. The guy said she didn't move for about three minutes. He thought she was dead. He said he was surprised that she stood up, grabbed her phone, and made a call. I grabbed her up, and took her to the ER. She had no broken bones, but lots of scrapes, scratches, bruises, and burns; and she walked out of there on her own.

Thank you, God, for sparing her life; it must be that she isn't done with your plan or purpose. Wow, to think God always watches over us and carries us to a safe place. Another lesson we learned was that golf carts weren't meant to go down steep hills. I think I would get off and walk—with age would come wisdom.

Never Stop

We got an invitation to move to Texas with my sister. She felt I needed a change from Oklahoma, and while I didn't see it, she did; and she opened her home up to us in Texas. So Michelle and I moved to Round Rock, Texas, a suburb of Austin, Texas. At that time I was looking for help, imagine that. The guy next door fit that bill, so within a year I was married to a man that financially could take care of Michelle and me. I knew we weren't a good fit, but I was worried and not sure how I was going to make it. (Just like my mom when we were children).

He was a nice man, but while he believed in God he didn't know him. At this time, Michael was living with his dad in Oklahoma City, and we shared custody. I would go up to Oklahoma every weekend to see Michael; it was six hours each way. When I got there, no one would be there. I would go back home, driving the six hours back, all upset and crying. This went on for one and a half years every weekend and some Wednesdays, but they never allowed me to see Michael at any time. We went back to court, and the judge ordered him to let me see my son.

Not only did I get to see my son, they had to meet me half way, which was in Dallas. I was grateful that this part was over, and I would be able to connect with my son again. The first few visits were unusual because they had to do supervised visits because people told the judge I was going to keep him. Michael was so young that his family told him the same story, so he was kind of scared of me. It didn't take very long, and Michael was comfortable around me again. I wish I could have spared him all of that, but you can't control what other people do, just how you react to it.

However one particular day Michael got into the car and was upset. I asked "him what was wrong," he said "Mom I need to ask you something."

I said, "Go ahead."

He said, "Grandma was talking to dad and she said well you think she would get it and quit after two years. You think she would just stop. What did she mean by that?"

I said, "Ahh, It doesn't matter."

Michael said, "No mom; tell me." I said, "Sweetie for a year and a half every week I would drive up to see you. Since I shared custody of you I would drive to see you, but you wouldn't be there. Your dad would not bring you all weekend and wouldn't let me see you."

They said, "You didn't want me."

I said, "No way, son, if I had been in a wheel chair I would have come. Nothing would have kept me from being a part of your life."

Michael started crying and I told him that I would do whatever it took to be a part of his life. Imagine, if you would, how God continues to want to be a part of our lives. We don't show up and don't seem to care whether he waits on us or not. But it never changes his pursuit of us, and how much time and energy he invests in you, because you are worth his time. Thank you Father for showing me you never quit on your children. Remember this, God wants you; he will stop at nothing to be a part of your life!

Sin Touches Everyone

Michelle was alone in the house, which never bothered me. Michelle was always very responsible. I was in Oklahoma watching my son play a football game. She called me to let me know she was home and in for the evening. I received a call at 2:15 a.m.; it was Michelle calling. She told me that a friend called needing help getting home. They had been drinking, and they didn't want to drive. I told her that was okay, but she was upset and tried to explain what had happened. I told her go to bed we would talk in the morning.

When I woke up, and regained my wits. I called Michelle. Michelle begins to explain that she got a call at 1:30 a.m. from a friend that needed a ride home. When she got there to pick him up, he had another friend that jumped in the back. As she was driving, she got pulled over by the police for having her high beams on. You see if you have your high beams on that is a signal that you're in trouble, and the police are trained to look for signs. They stopped her, and found out the kid in the back seat had a beer in his pocket. Michelle knew nothing about the liquor. The police gave Michelle a ticket for a minor in possession. She had to call another friend that was older. She was only seventeen and couldn't drive any one that had been drinking.

As the story unfolded Michelle was not looking good. She had to go to court, and I had to go with her. Michelle was out past her curfew, which was against the law. She snuck out of the house, didn't bother calling to tell me her plans. She got a ticket, had to go to court, and worst of all, she lost my trust.

Here is what went down. I had to take off work, so I could be there for my minor child. My boss had to take off work, which affects all the women who have appointments with her. They all had to reschedule, and make arrangements to come again at another time. Not to mention the doctors who have to pick up some of the patients, who have to be seen? Then my husband has to borrow $980 for the ticket from his parents, because we don't have that kind of money.

They are seniors so this puts a hurt on them for the month, because they live on a fixed income. Then if that isn't bad enough, Michelle will have a really bad ticket on her record, one she can't live down, and she doesn't even drink.

The day of court we had to stand before everyone. Michelle told the judge what happened. I made her apologize for her part in this ordeal. The judge said to me Mrs. Smith; it is not necessary for her to apologize. I said, oh yes, yes, it is. She has to know this is not the way we do things. You have so much to deal with, and she just added to your day.

Michelle apologized and the judge told her that she would have to go to a DUI class. I said seriously, she doesn't even drink, and she has to go to a DUI class? He told me I understand, but this is to give her information on the dangers of drinking and driving. Once she takes this class I will take the MIP off of her record. That could be another $150, but it was worth it not having that MIP on her record.

As we got home, it's my turn to lecture her, as if everything she has gone through isn't enough. Her heart was in the right place to help her friend; she just went about it the wrong way. I told Michelle that if she had been honest about everything she had done, she wouldn't have been in this situation. Next I told her that she is going to have to repay all of the money that we borrowed, and would be grounded until it was paid back. Summer was starting, so I knew it would take her a while to get it paid back. Next she was going to have to call or go over to everyone's house, and apologize for making him or her a part of her choices. I sent her to her room and called the boy's parents, and explained to them that I needed to talk to their son. They said they would be over in fifteen minutes. As they showed up I told Michelle to stay in her room.

As they came to the door I told his parents I would like to speak to him alone. So they went back out to their car, and he came in. I began by telling him that I was very proud of him for not drinking and driving, however I was not happy that in one night he had ruined Michelle's reputation. We had worked seventeen long years for her to have a good reputation, and he came along and in one night he destroyed everything we had built. I asked him why he didn't call his parents. He said because I didn't want to disappoint them by telling them that I had been drinking. I think I told him something like, you owe my daughter an apology, and she will not be able to hang around you until she is not grounded any longer.

Then I said if you ever need anything, you can call me and I will be happy to help no matter what time it is. I will be there for you. He started crying and told me how very sorry he was for everything that had happened. Then I got Michelle.

When she came around the corner, he said, "Michelle I am so sorry I got you into all this trouble, Please forgive me."

She looked at me and told me Mom; he doesn't have to do this. He told her yes, yes I do. She is right; we need to own what we do. He gave her a hug and left. Michelle went back to her room and sat on her bed. Michelle proceeded to sit on her bed for three days and stare at the walls. On the third day however she started yelling and slamming doors. I told Michael to take the door off of the hinges. Then I looked at her as she was going into the bathroom, and told her that if she slammed that door I would take it off of the hinges too. She would just have to figure how she was going to use the bathroom. The next day she asked if she could go get a job, which she did.

Then three weeks later she came in, and paid me everything she owed. I was thinking, goodness! I was hoping that it was going to take her all summer to get it paid back. But she looked at me and said, "I realized I could have sat around, but it wasn't going to get me anywhere. I chose to make everything right."

She then said, "Mom I am really sorry I did this, and I will earn your trust again."

I knew she had learned a valuable lesson, and would never repeat it again. Let's see how God was at work. He didn't allow Michelle to sneak out without being caught. He made sure Michelle had her high beams on to get stopped. He allowed the beer to be found. He made sure she would have to call me, so that the police would release her to go home. He showed Michelle how doing the wrong thing can affect so many lives, not just her own. He made her accountable for her choices. He allowed her to know that at any point she could ask forgiveness and change her outcome. He gave her a wonderful job that lasted her through high school that also kept her accountable to others besides me.

He helped Michelle restore trust to me and I loved her through the process. If you ask her today, she will tell you it was one of the most valuable lessons she ever learned. I thank you, Father, for teaching us, growing us, and loving us through all the times of our lives. Thank you, God, for watching over her that night, there is no telling what would have happened, but we will never know because you quietly walked through her life. Sin never just affects one's life; it has a way of touching so many others. Thank you Jesus, for leading by example, the way we always want to.

"But if we walk in the light, as he is in the light, we have fellowship with one another, and the blood of Jesus his Son cleanses us from all sin" (1 John 1:7, ESV).

Directed by God

I began working an after-school program at a daycare; I was in charge of making sure the older kids enjoyed their summer. Little did I know this was paving the way for me to work as a nanny? I interviewed and accepted a position with an OB-GYN doctor. Her daughter was eighteen months old and her son six weeks old. I was blessed to work with this family for over four years. I taught the kids everything, from potty training, to reading, writing, and sports.

One day the little girl had just had surgery on her throat. The parents told me that she would need to be watched very closely. If I saw any signs of bleeding I would need to call the doctor. Mom and dad had gone to work when the little girl started coughing, and seconds later I saw a little blood. So I dropped everything, and headed to hospital.

When I got there the ER was taking their time, but the girl was coughing up so much blood by now that she had lost a pint. She couldn't afford to lose any more blood. I called her mom. When the mom got there, I explained that it didn't seem to bother the emergency staff, or that she was so little and losing so much blood.

Within minutes they had to take her back to surgery, where they finally got the bleeding under control. Then after they came to recovery, the parents thanked me for having the wisdom to take her to the doctor instead of just waiting for someone to call back and let me know. They said I saved her life. It wasn't me; it was God who spared that little girl's life. It wasn't my wisdom it was God's who directed me what to do. God, thank you for saving her life and keeping me sensitive to hearing you speak.

"O LORD my God, I cried to you for help, and you have healed me" (Psalms 30:2, ESV).

Rain, Rain Go Away

Have you ever been in a place where when it rains it pours, and nothing but bad stuff keeps coming your way? One day my husband said something very rude and hateful to me. He told me that you're so fat no one could love you. I did something about that and lost weight. As I lost weight I got the confidence to say exactly what I needed to. I told him I was going to go to church. It was something I continually asked him to do with me— go to church. I was home one day and heard a knock on the door. It was a policeman asking for my husband, but he wasn't home.

They told me he had done something's that made me question his character. Then while I was at work, the family that I was a nanny for called me in, and told me I was being fired. I thought what is going on? The mom looked at me said you took my children out of school early, and have done it a couple of times. I looked at the dad, and he said nothing. You see he was the one that told me to take the kids out of school, and take them over to his parents' house. I would only take them out of school when he asked me too, because he was running late or visiting with co-workers. Either way, he didn't cover me. So they gave me my pay, and sent me on my way. I didn't even get to say good-bye to the kids. I was hurt and upset, but as I walked outside the dad came up to me, and said "I am so sorry Brenda" and gave me a hug.

Now he has to live with the fact that he was doing something behind his wife's back. Someone else had to pay the price for what he was doing. Now I'm getting another divorce, lost my job, having to move, then find out my husband has not paid taxes for over eight years so we owe the IRS $25,000. My life was pretty much in the toilet, except I am going to church again. We sold our house, we paid the debts, and then we divided the assets.

Then as God always does, He gave me a job, a good job at IBM. I was making three times what I was making as a nanny; thank you, Jesus! Then I got a new car; thank you, Jesus! Then I was able to buy a brand new house, thank you, Jesus! Imagine being restored to even better…Wow! It's funny when you finally decide to follow after God the enemy quickly tries to see just how serious you are and throws everything at you to discourage you. Once again, thank you, Jesus, for all your blessings, but mostly your love that sees us through everything.

"O Lord of hosts, blessed is the one who trusts in you" (Psalms 84:12, esv).

It was at this time I was very much living in the flesh. I was skinny, in my early forties, and didn't mind dating. Trust me when I say this: having the wrong kind of attention is still attention, and it will get you into trouble. I must have dated around thirty guys, not bragging…I was just looking for that one that God had for me. Well, at least, that was my excuse. So I wasn't going to church much because I stayed out and entertained.

When Sunday morning rolled around I slept. I remember this one morning I was going to visit another man when God said "No more! Go to Church!"

I said, "I don't know which one to go to."

He said "That one!" as I was driving by this church.

Now I must have driven by that church a thousand times, no kidding, but I never saw it. I went in and sat down. As the music played, I knew I was home. When they gave the invitation I went down and repented, asking God to forgive me, which he did. Now it was time for me to forgive myself. You see God is quick to forgive you, but you have to live with the consequences, and the time you wasted. I have learned that I hate wasting time, because it is so precious, and we can't get it back. To think we could have done so much more if we had only been where God wanted us.

Like me, some of us are slow and take a while to figure it out. I'm grateful God's mercy and grace is new every day. I met wonderful friends at church. We stayed connected so that we had special times every week that we got together. I love how God shows me through his people how much he cares about us. One time I was going to visit Michael in Oklahoma and on the way back I called one of my Christian brothers to talk to him so I wouldn't fall asleep. As I told him how tired I was, he said he would meet me in Dallas. That is exactly what he did.

He met me in Dallas and had a car dolly and hooked up my little bug, and pulled me all the way back while I slept. Now that is brotherly love, caring for one another, reaching out, and showing God's love. I will never forget that as long as I live. To me, that was one of the kindest acts I have ever witnessed. Thank you God for allowing me to have wonderful, caring, friends and for allowing me to be one!

"Therefore welcome one another as Christ has welcomed you, for the glory of God" (Romans 15:7, esv).

Take It for a Spin

Michael was visiting me for the summer. It was the summer he would turn sixteen. The last time he was here we got him his beginners permit, and he was excited about it. Michael was excited because he was getting to hang out with me, and his sister. Also while Michael was in Austin, he decided to take a job. He decided that he was going to get a job at a tanning salon, and he did. On his birthday he got his driver's license, which was very important for any sixteen-year-old. He was going to church and loving every minute of it. He would even go to the men's fellowship with the older men. One man stopped me at church one Sunday, and told me that Michael was such a blessing to the men's fellowship. He prays with everyone, no matter what the age. Michael was only fifteen but he thought it was important to pray for your brother in Christ. He prayed for anyone and it didn't matter if they were fifty years old.

Needless to say he was the youngest person there, but then anointing knows no age. Michael would come up to my work during the day, and then go to his work in the afternoon. One day we decided that he needed to look for a car. He had saved $500 so we began looking.

Guy walked in, and asked what we were doing? We told him that we were looking for a car for Michael. Do you know if anyone is selling one cheap, because we don't have much to spend? He looked at us and smiled. Then he said "I have a Ford Escort; nothing fancy, but a good dependable car. Let me ask my wife tonight, and I will let you know what we can do about it."

The next day we came back to work. Guy told us that he talked to his wife, and they thought that Michael was a fine young man, and that they wanted to give the car to Michael. My son went 'what', are you kidding me? Michael's eyes started tearing up and he gave Guy a hug and said, "thank you, thank you, thank you."

He looked at him and said, "Go check it out." So we went outside and sure enough there it was, he handed the keys to Michael and said, "Take it for a spin. Wait, I forgot to fill it up with gas; here is $40 to fill it up." Then he signed the title over to Michael and me. Wow, to think God would send someone our way and give us a car! Thank you, thank you, thank you, my words are never enough.

Need for Keys

This was a particularly busy week; we had an audit at work, which meant long hours for me. I was also busy with church things and visiting people, so I got home late. I am in the habit of putting my keys on the kitchen counter so I won't forget them. I am notorious for losing my keys anytime, anywhere. That particular night I walked up stairs, and realized I still had my keys in my pocket…goodness! I wasn't going back downstairs so I just put them on the banister by the stairs. I crawled into bed, and I was out like a light. It was about 3:00 a.m. when I woke up, and my mouth was so dry I was smacking my mouth trying to get some moisture back into it, and it wasn't working.

This went on for about fifteen minutes; I was so tired I wasn't getting up to get a drink. Then out of nowhere my car alarm went off, I jumped to my feet, and started running downstairs. As I started to head downstairs I realized that my keys where right there, so I grabbed them and hit my panic button on my keys. As I looked down, a cat had jumped on my car and set the alarm off.

It was then I said thank you Jesus! God knew I was going to need to get up at 3:00 a.m., so my keys were right where I could get them. Then God knew I was going to need a drink of water, but too tired to keep up, he made the alarm go off. God knew I needed the rest, so he didn't want my sleep to be interrupted. As I walked, back I got a drink of water and crawled back into bed.

Thank you Jesus for knowing what I was going to need, and providing everything even to the last detail. You never cease to amaze me Lord!

"What is man that you are mindful of him, and the son of man that you care for him" (Psalms 8:4, ESV).

Plans for Good

Have you ever said something, and the moment it came out of your mouth, you knew it was wrong? I had just gotten back from church camp, and the pastor asked me to pray over the service in the morning. I was so scared I couldn't move, but all I could think was no way, not me. Out the words came "nah." This was a big deal back in the early seventies because first I was a girl. Second, they didn't allow girls to even say anything on the pulpit. I was also very young, which young people were not even seen during a service. We also were a Baptist church, which made me know that others might look down on me. I wasn't worthy of standing before them. It was the early seventies and everyone knew their place. I felt bad after I said no, but I couldn't take it back. I never realized that God was trying to do something in the church, and I could have been used. After that I was asked to be the youth director, but turned it down as well. I couldn't get over the fact that I was a girl in a man's world.

Coming back from church camp, I was asked to read scripture. This time I didn't turn it down. My nerves were on edge, believe it or not. Those of you that know me know I am not shy at all. I had the most difficult time standing before a crowd. I remember reading about how God cares for the lilies in the valley, and the birds of the air, how much more will he care for us. Then I said after I read the verse I like knowing God will take care of me. I hurried off stage and went and sat down. After church nobody made me feel bad, in fact most of them came up, and said what a great job I had done. After that I went to a bigger church, and then finally settled at a church of four thousand. I ended up speaking before thousands, and while I might have been nervous I was more concerned with doing what God wanted. God was preparing me for more. I went from a hundred to a thousand and in the same day to millions.

God always wants us to stretch ourselves to doing our best. I also got to be used as youth director for several churches, even though I was a girl! I even got the opportunity to pray at my childhood church again. This time it was thirty-five years later at my grandmother's funeral. God woke me up at 1:00 a.m. telling me I was going to pray over Grandma's funeral, and all I could say was, "no!"

So, I wrestled with God telling me yes you are…and this is what you're going to say. I kept refusing, until 4 a.m. The moment I said yes to God, I will pray. I was finally able to rest. When I got to church I told our pastor that I was supposed to pray over the funeral, and he told me please feel free. I know it's what your grandma would like. The funeral was special, and I got to pray for the last time over my grandmother. While some of the men thought it was their job, everyone said they were very moved by the prayer. I hope you caught the fact that I said, I got to pray instead of had to pray.

Wow, God can transform lives in so many ways if we just yield to him. Thank you, God for continually calling me and not taking a "NO" for an answer. We never know the plans God has for us, but they are for good!

"Many are the plans in the mind of a man, but it is the purpose of the LORD that will stand" (Proverbs, 19:2 ESV).

I Want That

There was a time that I wanted to get a scooter so badly; it was all I could think about. I rode a scooter when I was on vacation, and I was hooked. It was only a small 50CC so I couldn't really enjoy all that a scooter had to offer. I mean when I went up a hill I would literally have to push it up with both of my feet, because it didn't have enough power to get me up the hill. I wasn't the only one doing it either. After a few months of talking to my husband, I finally convinced him too buy me a scooter. I started out with a 250CC while it had the get up and go; it still didn't have enough power to climb any of the hills, we had round our place. I would start out at sixty miles an hour, by the time I climbed a hill I was doing maybe twenty.

My husband was worried I would get ran over, so we went to buy a bigger scooter, a 600 CC. Now let me tell you I never paid attention to the road until I was on the scooter. The things we take for granted when we are in a car, you don't do that when you're in a scooter/motorcycle.

For instance, if there is a groove in the street from workers it will pull you into it, and you feel hopeless until you can get out; if there are larger rocks, trash, glass and rubber on the road it can cause you to wreck.

I never felt as comfortable as I would like, driving the scooter, because the fear was always there. One time we decided we would take a trip to Oklahoma City from Austin, Texas it was a six-hour trip by car, but double that on a motorcycle. We started off with the day being nice and sunny, a little windy just another thing to be concerned for. Then as we pulled into Waco it started to rain. We had to stop for rain gear now. I looked back now, and think to myself why in the world didn't I just turn around, and go back since I was only an hour and a half away. I didn't though we kept going, after the rain slowed down, not stopped but slowed down. It was cold and miserable. The rain on the road made for just one more thing to be concerned for.

By the time we hit Hillsboro, I was nervous, and scared of what was around the corner. Every time we stopped, I breathed a sigh of relief. By the time we crossed over in to Oklahoma, it was two o' clock in the morning; we were still over two hours away. I felt we were never going to get there. The rain began to pour again, and I never wanted to get on that silly scooter again. We pushed forward, and made it to Oklahoma City about 4:30 a.m. or twelve hours after we left Austin. I forgot to tell you how sore my bottom was, it was numb from being on the road so long.

Now this is no the mode of transportation I would recommend to everyone to get around on, but it's what I wanted. The next day after we rested, it was time to head back. The weather was going to be perfect, and we were heading out early in the morning so we wouldn't be on the road in the evening. I was grateful that we each were riding bikes, so we were more visible. I was shaking in my boots. At one point I even told my friends, I wished we could just load these up, and drive them back. My brother offered to take us back, but there was something in me that wanted to say, I drove from Oklahoma City to Austin and back. Now how silly is that, wanting to be able to say you drove so far on a motorcycle.

We got on the road and headed back. I was nervous the whole way, the wind threw me around several times, and the road was slick enough that it made the bike hard to handle. We got off of the highway on our exit, and I was never so happy to be in one place again. I should have had a lot of fun, but I was so uneasy about the whole trip, I couldn't. I wanted the scooter gone, and I didn't care if I ever rode it again.

Thank you, Jesus, you allowed us to have what we wanted. But sometimes it's only a good idea, not a good plan, and it's never too late to turn around.

"Those whom I love, I reprove and discipline, so be zealous and repent" (Revelation 3:19, esv).

Service With a Smile

The church had made an announcement that if anyone would like to volunteer to help feed the homeless, please let them know. You could go to downtown Austin, and help a young man making a difference with the homeless. I decided I would go, not knowing what I could do, but I did want to help.

When I got there everyone was preparing lunch. They asked me to jump in and help. As people started to come, it was refreshing to see everyone waiting on our guest. The volunteers would sit down beside the homeless and started talking. A few minutes later someone stepped up, and started singing songs. It was so cool to see everyone lifting his or her hands in praise to God. Being homeless I figured they had no reason, in my eyes, to be singing praises. Most of them were hungry, tired, lonely, and in need of many things.

After the singing, one man stepped out, and started talking about his addictions, his lifestyle, and why he ended up on the streets. Surprisingly, he wasn't an unhappy person. He recognized why he was where he was, and he was very grateful that God was restoring him to someplace better. He also talked about the fact that people cared enough to encourage him and help him get a clean set of clothes. He was now starting his first job on Monday. He talked about how much he realized how bad his life had gotten. That he needed Jesus, and that God has a plan for his life. He thanked everyone there for adding to his world. I was hooked.

Though these homeless people were not in the best of places, they could come and get physically fed, emotionally cared for, and spiritually filled. This was a light in their dark world. They were so grateful that people didn't look at them like trash, but treated them like treasures. I was blessed to see so many came to know Jesus, got off of the streets, got jobs, and be given a second chance. Isn't that what all of us really need anyhow? I was allowed to mentor several families, adults, and even children. My life was richer for the experience and I never looked at people on the streets in the same way. Thank you, Father, for showing me that we can praise you in any circumstance because it is never what it looks like.

My Sweetie, Our RV, and Me

I was living with my friend but was looking for somewhere else to live. Shopping as we girls do, I come across a deal on the Internet? It was a fifth wheel, and a truck for what was a sweet deal. I made a deal with the man and his wife to make payments, so after six weeks it was paid in full. I also got to leave the fifth wheel at the RV Park it was at. The RV Park was only five miles from my job. Excited about saving money and about the area I was in. I was only five minutes from church, shopping, and work was great!

My son-in-law helped put new carpet in it, and a new refrigerator, plus other things; it was shaping up nicely. At this time, I had not been dating for about four years, and had no intentions of ever dating again. I was on the Internet sharing my testimony wherever and whenever I could. One particular evening I was sharing with one guy about Jesus, and he was trying to share Jesus with me. When we figured out we were both trying to witness to each other. Since we knew Jesus we just had to laugh. We exchanged phone numbers so we could share our stories, and encourage one another in our Christian walk.

He told me that he was an associate pastor of a church near him. I told him where I went to church, and how I liked to volunteer for different things. I also told him I was living in an RV, and he thought it was cool. I thought wow; he doesn't even care where I live; that's neat! Our conversation started out just wanting to kind of get acquainted, but six hours later and at 3 a.m., we finally hung up. This went on for two or three weeks then we decided we needed to meet.

The first time I met Ron I looked at him and said "you wear JESUS well." It was one of the highest compliments I ever paid anyone. He was a Godly man that loved Jesus. I did look at his shoes, because I am a Nike girl. He had said don't look at my shoes they aren't Nike. He told me if you couldn't get it at Wal-Mart, you didn't need it. Our first date was the best ever; we got him new Nike shoes, so now he could be seen with me...

We went to church, and waited for the doors to open. We just sat in the car, and listened to music, sang (not that I can sing, but God did say to make a joyful noise, which I did). Then into church, and then to eat, it was the perfect date. We met in March and were married in August by his pastor. The difference between my first two marriages, and this one, was that I never understood what being married was all about. It is a covenant between you, God, and the person you are going to spend your life with.

Thank you, Lord, for the man you had for me all along. It's been seven years, but it feels like it's only been days. Imagine when God is allowed to work in your lives how truly blessed we are. It's a happily ever after situation just like in my dreams—our RV Ron and me.

We Belong to YOU

We had only been married a short while, when both of our jobs in Austin seemed to be dwindling away. We decided that we would like to work together. We started looking into jobs for couples, and came across a house-parenting job in Tucson, Arizona. I had just been laid off from IBM, and Ron was only a temp at his job. We figured this was as good a time as any to make our move. We contacted the ministry there. After several phone interviews, and a thorough background search, they hired us sight unseen. They even helped pay for moving costs, so we were on our way to Tucson, Arizona.

We had two cars, and Ron had told me that I needed to sell my car. I didn't want to part with my cool Scion XB. On Saturday, I got up and God told me to sell my car. I said I only have two days before we leave; God said I only need one. I listed it on Craigslist, and a guy called me an hour after I listed it. They gave me $10,000 cash for it. I paid the loan off, and still had over $5000 to hold us over. God knew he wanted me to ride to Tucson with Ron.

I wasn't going to need it, so God made sure it was sold just that fast. The kids came over Sunday night, and packed us up. That Monday we would be headed west. We arrived in Tucson the next day, and it was just beautiful. I had to remind myself I was in the desert. We were put into a home that was just as gorgeous. It was a two-story house with all the amenities that you could imagine, plus a view that was spectacular, with mountains all around. We went from living in a RV to a five-bedroom house. We were given a job sight unseen, selling my car in one day, making more in salary, and best of all getting to work together.

God was really blessing us, and it was an exciting time because we were entering another ministry, where we could touch more lives. It was at this time we were getting e-mails from Germany, telling us that they had more information on Ron's birth mom. Ron was adopted in Germany at the age of five. While I had been laid off for two months, I decided I would look up any information I could, and find out about his birth parents.

I had a wonderful correspondence with a girl named Gabrielle. She had found out his real name, birthplace, and even his birth certificate. We were excited every time we got e-mail from her. We had only been in Tucson for about six weeks. We received another e-mail from Gabrielle, but this one was BIG! It said, I have located your real birth mother, and she gave her name, phone number, and even her address. The address was no other than in Tucson; we were twenty-five minutes away from where she lived. Ron was gone, but I called her to ask her if she had a son and daughter, and if she had lived in Germany.

I continued with did she have children she gave up for adoption, she said yes to everything. By that time, Ron walked into the house. I told him you're not going to believe this, but your birth mother is on the phone. Ron smiled, and even though he was shocked he started talking to her. A few days later Ron went to meet her. They talked about his family and hers and we took pictures, it was too cool to actually see them together. Ron even got to meet his sister that he knew nothing about. This story doesn't have a happy ending, because a few weeks later Ron's biological mom came back, and said he wasn't her son. Even though he was, she must have felt so guilty, because she gave up two kids, and kept one.

As Ron left her house, he was upset and told me I cannot talk right now; I have to talk to my Daddy. By the time he got home he was better though. It was tough to be rejected two times by the same person, but Ron never was without a mom that loved him, and poured into his life.

We thank you, Father, for always being there for us, for showing us our value and worth when the world tells us different.

"For you did not receive the spirit of slavery to fall back into fear; but you have received the Spirit of adoption as sons, by whom we cry, 'Abba! Father!'" (Romans 8:5, esv)

Finding Your Home

We were so blessed to have so many children come through our house. One of them was a girl, named Destiny that had just a few little unusual habits. She was on loan to us from Mexico along with her sister. Her family did everything they could to get her into a better situation. The parents couldn't take care of Destiny and her sister, so they took them across the border. It took them almost a year to be found out by the department of human services, and they didn't get to stay together. One of them ended up in foster home, and Destiny came to live with us at the age of fourteen. I can't even imagine what she was doing before she got to us, but she was definitely ready for a place to call home.

She told us that before she got to our place, she was with some family members that would throw some food out the door for her, and her sister. They maybe ate once a day; and yes it landed in the dirt, but they ate it anyway. They slept under the porch, and just as long as they didn't make any noise they could stay, but things happened that forced them to have to leave. Fortunately, the state caught them, and placed them in good homes. Destiny for some reason didn't like her food too much, which was no big deal. We were happy to accommodate her food to make her feel loved, so that she felt she belonged.

Destiny also didn't like eating food with metal, because it bothered her teeth. She preferred plastic utensils. We even got her heavy utensils that were pink, because that was her favorite color. She also was unable to sleep with other children because of things in her past, so we put her by herself in a separate bedroom. God worked it out, so that she never had to share with anyone, which made it comfortable for her. Destiny was one of the first kids that saw the need for God in her life, and embraced it with her whole heart. This really helped her, because she tended to have bouts of depression. One evening someone in the house decided to pick on everyone including Destiny.

That frustrated Destiny, and because she was a 'runner' her first reaction was to run. That is what she did whenever she was upset. Our only recourse was to call the police when the children ran away. So we called the police, and informed them that we had a runaway. It was around 8:30 p.m. and we were concerned because that's when the havalina and Gila monsters come out. Havalina's are like small wild pigs with tusks and Gila monsters are large lizards that are very deadly. The animals only came out at night, so we really never had a problem with kids running away at night; they were all in for the night. Destiny must have forgotten that when she took off, but as we went outside she was standing in the middle of the field. She was about the length of a football field away. She was just standing there. I yelled at her to come back. She said nothing, but I could tell she was scared and upset.

The police came but just turned around and left, because she could be seen...so she wasn't technically a runaway. We all went inside, because there was nothing we could do, and we were hoping she might return if we left her alone. It was about twenty minutes later when she came back in the house. Destiny went to her room, and said nothing. When I went down to talk to her she was crying. I asked her why she was so upset.

She said, "I had nowhere to go. If I ran I would have nothing. It's hard to accept that I have no choices. This is it for me."

If she had run she had nowhere to go, and that was heartbreaking for her. I realized it was a defining moment for her, but there was freedom for her as well. She had people that loved her, accepted her, and supported her in every way. She stopped running after that. We thank you, God that she found her home on earth, and in heaven, and she made her peace with it.

All I have is a buck

The first house we trained in, we did relief for the regular houseparent's. We took care of the house, when the houseparent's had their days' off. They had nine kids, mostly around eight; one as young as six and one sixteen. This particular house was in need of a little TLC. We challenged the kids to help get the house more organized. The kids weren't really into it until I told them I would reward them for their efforts.

One thing the parents gave us before they left was these brand new bags of socks. We could give the kids socks when they asked. I thought it was peculiar, but I said okay and went on. As I was doing laundry, I understood why she had brand new socks. There must have been about two hundred pairs of socks in the laundry room, ready to be matched-up.

When the kids came home from school we helped them with their homework. Larry at six years old was excited when he got home from school. He told me he wanted to go to school the next day and get a book since they were having a book fair. He asked me if I would give him some money. I told him I knew of a way he could make some. When the kids were done with their studies, I told them there were socks that needed to be matched up. For every pair they matched up we would give them a dime.

Larry said I can't do that!

I said that is how you're going to make some money for the book fair.

Quickly two of the older kids ran unto the playroom, where all the socks were laid out on a table. As each one grabbed a match I would say Tommy has ten cents. Sally has twenty cents. Bobby has ninety cents. As the kids kept digging some of the amounts got up to two and three dollars.

Then little Larry decides that he just might like to earn some money too so he ran in there. We had six kids out of nine grabbing socks, and matching them; it was actually very fun for them.

One kid ended up with $6.00, one with $5.50, one with $4.20, one with $3.10, one with $2.20 and little Larry got $1.00. We ended up with 220 pairs of matched socks and even though it cost us $22 but it was well worth it.

The kids were so excited, because they had never gone to a book fair, and they were ready for this one. The next morning Larry was sitting on the couch ready to go to school. He looked at Ron, and told him all I got is a buck.

Ron said, "Well you have clothes don't you?"

He said, "Yes I do have clothes, and a buck."

Ron then said, "You have shoes don't you?"

He said, "Yes I do have shoes, clothes, and a buck."

Ron then said, "You have a backpack don't you?"

He said, "Yes, yes I do; I have a backpack, clothes, shoes, and a buck, but that's all I have."

Then Larry told Ron, "Well, I am not going to school with only a buck."

Ron looked at him and said, "Then give me the buck!"

Larry said, "What?" He then grabbed his backpack and headed for the door. Just a side note, Larry did come home from school that day, and was able to get a book even with just a buck! It's so neat when everything comes together, but even greater when we see the results of doing the right thing. The house looked great when the regular houseparent's came back, and the kids took pride in the way the house looked from that point on. Thank you Father for allowing us to encourage the kids, and inspire them to want to take care of what you have given them.

"Therefore encourage one another and build one another up, just as you are doing" (1 Thessalonians 5:11, ESV).

Marriage Made to Serve

Have you ever come to the place where you realize that this is what you're meant to do with your lives? Michael and his wife Ashley had always liked working with children. From as early as fourteen years old, they both always enjoyed being with children. Michael worked with me at church, Sunday school, church camps, and helping as youth director. Ashley found herself always wanting to babysit, and play with all the kids in the neighborhood. With Michael and Ashley, it always felt right when they were around kids. When they got married both worked at several different jobs, with no fulfillment, just working for the money.

However they hardly ever saw each other, which they didn't like. When they got the opportunity to work as associate houseparent's in Arizona, they loved it. But it wasn't their time, so they once again took other jobs, but weren't passionate about them. Ashley decided at this time that if she was going to work she wanted to make a difference with kids. Ashley took nanny jobs, and enjoyed her time with them, but she still wasn't getting to see Michael.

Michael and Ashley finally came to a place where they decided that they wanted to work together. They enjoyed working together, and they loved making a difference in children's lives. They got serious, and only applied for positions that allowed them the opportunity.

Wow, to think they actually got paid for doing what God created them to do, it was such a blessing. God gave them a peace as long as they are working with children. It was such a thrill to see them finally figure out their life's work, and they were only twenty-two. Don't we wish we could have figured out what we were called to do at such a young age? Watching children grow, learn, and become all they are meant to be has its own rewards. It was neat seeing them as they took their place. I couldn't imagine them doing anything else with their lives because this is what they were meant to do. To think they get to help re-write a child's future is incredible, and to think the children are helping to re-write theirs. Children are gifts from God. How we help teach, encourage, and love them is our gift back to God. Children are our greatest assets.

All Michael and Ashley wanted to do was make sure they could make a difference one kid at a time. Our future is not defined by our past, and helping children find their future is very rewarding. Michael and Ashley want to give them the best of themselves. It's what the children deserve, and they can do no less. Thank you Father for shaping them apart, and putting them together, and giving them a purpose so they affect so many others!

Gracie Is Home

While in Tucson, we met wonderful caring adults, and one of them was Dr. Turner. She worked with the teenage mothers, and what a blessing she was. We became the best of friends, because she was kind, loving, thoughtful, and compassionate. Just like me! NOT. I was drawn to her gentle spirit and wisdom from God. She was all alone, and in a house full of teenage mothers and independent girls. As we got to know her she would encourage us, and give us a HUG. Dr. Turner was heaven sent, in a place where most of us were overlooked. She managed to make each and every one of us feel special.

When she met Ron, she said, well nice to meet you Pastor Ron.

Ron said it sure was nice to be recognized as a pastor since God had spoken that into his life a long time ago. Whenever Ron needed some words of wisdom he would call her. He valued her input. We would always try, and get together when one of us were off. We would have some fellowship time at Denny's Restaurant. We loved on her as much as she loved on us. Our time was cut short—the state of Arizona could not pay for their childcare facilities. We had to take another position.

Dr. Turner cried when left we were her only friends there. God was working things out. One day Dr. Turner saw a picture of our puppy.

She said I'm so happy you got my new puppy.

I said what are you talking about?

She said God is bringing me a puppy and I'm going to call her Gracie.

That's funny because that was her name Gracie. The moment she said that the puppy was hers. I knew it was too, but I just told her, when she has puppies I will make sure you get one.

She said, "No, I will make sure you have one; this one is mine."

Sure enough the place that we were going didn't allow dogs, so we had to get rid of her. I guess Dr. Turner knew better than I did. I thank you Jesus, for allowing our family to be a part of hers. God knew she needed a loving little Gracie, which would add to her life. Thank you for allowing us to give just a little into her life; it doesn't compare to how much she gives into ours! To think Gracie is touching her life while she is blessing so many others makes me smile!

Sharing Their Story

We were at our new houseparent position. We were working with boys that had different reasons for being there: gangs, drugs, truancy, runaways, and parents are not able to control them. It was very stressful since we had three different gangs living in the one house. We met our neighbors Rob and Cindy. We were very excited that they were Christians, and they offered to help anyway they could. The boys proved to be typical boys; they needed structure, compassion, and love. We were privileged to see ten boys come to have a relationship with God. We had wonderful devotions, and the boys always surprised me with how deep they could go. An opportunity to go to summer camp with all the boys came up, so we jumped on it. The drive was three hours away.

Cindy and I drove one van while the guys drove another one. We had mostly all the supplies for four homes. God was working this out, because Cindy and I got to talk, and share the whole way down to camp.

As we started to talk, Cindy expressed how great it was that I could share the gospel with anyone, and how bold I was in doing it. I began to ask her about her testimony. Cindy told me, I'm not sure what it would be! I began sharing my testimony with her, so that she would have an idea of what it might sound like.

I told her that there were three things you look for in a testimony:

(1) What your life was like before Jesus,
(2) Where you were at when God drew you,
(3) What your life was like after coming to know Jesus.

As we talked, I shared with her how when Jesus comes in there is always a change. Then she talked about how she started going to church with Rob when they first met. She didn't want to go to church, because there were lots of hypocrites, and she didn't need or want to be around them. Rob invited her to church, and told her that if she didn't like it she wouldn't have to come again. Rob was okay with the fact that she believed in God, and that was good enough. Cindy said Rob wasn't as strong in his walk at the time, but just happy they believed the same way. Cindy went to her first service and liked it; so she kept going. Before she knew it, she was going every week.

One week while she was there the pastor asked if there was anyone that would like to accept Jesus, and she did.

She said "I knew I wanted to give my life to God, and do as much as I could while I was in this life because life is too short."

I told her that God would send people her way that needed her testimony—for example, people who had been hurt by the church, also people that didn't see the need for God. Then I began to share with her how to share the gospel, and how to lead someone in the prayer of salvation. We practiced the rest of the way to camp, until she was comfortable with every aspect from sharing her testimony, to sharing the gospel, as well as, the prayer of Salvation. It was so cool to see someone get so excited about sharing his or her faith. When we got back to campus it was less than three days, and Cindy had got to share her testimony with someone. They wanted a relationship with Christ, and she had the privilege of leading them. She was on fire, and I couldn't be happier.

In less than a year she had been privileged to see seven people accept Jesus. The neatest thing was that when I asked her how many times she thought she had got to share with others, she said I can't tell you; it's been so many times I couldn't count! Wow! To think someone so timid, shy, and never knowing she had that all inside of her. To go from there to someone that takes every opportunity to tell her story, the one that God gave her. Thank you God for giving us all a story, but especially for helping us to find our voice, and being able to be bold enough to share it!

"Go therefore and make disciples of all nations, baptizing them in the name of the Father and of the Son and of the Holy Spirit" (Matthew 28:19, esv).

Never in Need

Ron was going to school online, he is a lifetime learner. He tells everyone that he doesn't want to pay back the loan, that's why he keeps going. Honestly, he loves to learn, especially about God. Anyway, it was at this time that we tithed into a ministry, we knew God was using. We love to tithe because it's an opportunity to do several things. First, we love God, and recognize he is everything to us. Second, it is being obedient. Third, we want to see lives changed, because people will hear the gospel. Fourth, we want to be blessed, and not cursed.

Laying all that aside how could we not want to give just a portion back to God, who gives us everything. The Bible talks about how we are to prove him, and see if he will not pour out a blessing we cannot contain. Here is just one way we tithed, and God poured out. We had tithed $1000, and within a week our truck broke down. Now let me share this, we were on the highway, and it started cutting out, so we headed for an auto mechanic. They weren't open but just next door was a Ford dealership, which is what we were driving. So, we went next door just in time for the truck not to start again. We could have walked home it was only a mile away, but a friend from campus came, and picked us up.

The dealership called, and told us what was wrong with it. They were telling us it was going to cost $4500 because the truck was out of warranty. Then the next day they called us back, and told us that the truck had a recall for the very thing that was wrong, so all the costs would be covered under the Factory Recall. Thank you, God! It broke down again a week after we got it back, and once again it was another recall item, so they ended up replacing the whole engine before it was all said and done. The cost to us was absolutely nothing.

The next thing was when we thought we would buy this house in a very small quaint town in north Nebraska. We put down $3000 that was non-refundable, but it turned out that we weren't supposed to get it, so God made sure we got all our money back, thank you God.

Here are more stories how God blessed us. We were looking for a couch, because we had moved and sold the other one. It was cheaper not to move the current couch, but sell it and get another one when we got to where we were going. I'm picky when it comes to couches, and my shoes. It's a big deal. I was living in one apartment and went through three couches before I finally got the one I liked. I found a couch listed on

Craigslist. I love how I find so many things on Craigslist; it's like a giant garage sale one piece at a time. The lady said she had the couch custom-made, and her husband didn't like it so he wanted it gone. We got there, and the plastic was still on it, so was the sales slip of $3455.00. The couch was the perfect color, fabric, and comfort, and she only wanted $500 for it. All I had was $400 but she took it! Thank you, God, for a couch designed just for me. Wow, to think God does all this and more. He's just waiting for the opportunity to show you.

Peaceful Passage

We were at peace going to Baptist Children's Home. Upon our arrival, we had to have our driver's license changed from Nebraska to Oklahoma. We had to have two forms of identification (ID). Ron didn't have a passport or birth certificate, but we did have his old naturalization papers. We had to go to the DMV to give them all the information we had on his naturalization papers. They said they couldn't accept those forms of ID, because they were too old. They gave us a phone number to call a particular lady, and see if she could approve him getting his license. We talked to her and she had us fax over what we had, and then she called us back. She called homeland security, and told us to go to their Website to fill out the forms. Then she said it would cost us $400. We thought oh wonderful, because at least we will have his naturalization papers. He was never able to get his naturalization papers the whole time he had been in the United States. We filled out the forms, sent them in along with the check.

A week later they informed us that he would be cleared for his certification, but that the fee was being waived. Sweet! Coming to a new job, and having to get a new driver's license forced us to go to a place to meet a lady who for no reason went out of her way to help us get Ron's naturalization papers. Oh, and the really cool thing is we didn't have the money; we needed the cash to pay the car payment. There was only a window of opportunity to get a legal document approved. While we sent off for the naturalization papers, we also sent off for his passport. When one office called us to verify something we had both offices working on getting the papers pushed through.

The passport approved Ron because the naturalization office said he was getting those naturalization papers as well. We got Ron's passport back. Thank you, Jesus, for allowing that to come through. It has been such a struggle to get his information in line for him to be able to show his citizenship. But God is making a way, where everything else has failed. We now can go get his Oklahoma driver's license since we now have two proofs of identification, thank you, Father. I know God is lining everything up because he is opening a door for us to minister in other countries. Thank you, Father, that your timing is perfect and as you make a way we only need to walk it out.

Proverbs 3:4-6 ESV

"So shalt thou find favor and good understanding In the sight of God and man. Trust in Jehovah with all thy heart, And lean not upon thine own understanding: In all thy ways acknowledge him, And he will direct thy paths."

Making a Way

We picked up our mattresses and kitchen stuff on Thursday in Austin, and left for Tucson Arizona. It was supposed to rain everyday we were gone. We arrived in Tucson on Wednesday evening at 4:00 p.m., and we never got rained on. Our mattress was in perfect condition. No big deal to you, but we didn't have the money to replace it. Not to mention God allows our stuff to last longer than they should.

It was moving day. We finally got to move into our cottage, but we didn't have a couch or a bed yet. I looked on Craigslist again, and started sending out e-mails. I prayed the night before asking God to give me this exact bed. I waited on the call, but in the morning never got it. I found a couch and chair for $180. I called, and they said it was available, thank you, Jesus!

As we were getting ready to go, one of the cottages called and asked if our youth could hang out with theirs for the day. What a blessing, we didn't have to worry about watching the youth in our cottage. Off we went to get our couch. When we got there the couch was amazing, beautiful, and comfortable, and a chaise chair to go with it. Someone else was coming to get it in the next five minutes, but God wanted to bless us with it. By the way the couch and chair had cost $2,200. The couple only used it in the sitting area of their house, so it hardly got used, that's why it looked like new.

When we pulled up in the driveway my phone rang, as I answered it. I was surprised that it was the lady with the exact bed I prayed about… Thank you, God. God kept me busy, so I wouldn't look for another bed since he knew what I wanted. Otherwise I would have settled for something else; but his timing was perfect.

"Delight yourself in the LORD, and he will give you the desires of your heart" (Psalms 37:4, ESV).

More than Enough

At our staff meeting, we told the staff that we didn't have a refrigerator, and one of the ladies said she had one. All we had to do was come get it, Praise God! She also said she had a dresser we could have. Guess what? It was white so it matched my bed. That's the kind of God we serve right down to the last thing, especially for us ladies we like things to match.

Imagine all this and we pay nothing for it. When we were finished with the staff meeting; our director said a man was donating things down at the garage. All we had to do was go see if there was anything we would like. Naturally there was a brand new microwave, a table, and four chairs, and a love seat. Now don't get me wrong, I didn't need the love seat but it was perfect for the cottage. God always blows me away even when I least expect it. But then, like our associate says, he loves us and is always watching out for us.

I am so amazed at how fast God moves when you align yourself to where he wants you. I am humbled by just the thought of him. Thank you, God! We were getting a new girl in our cottage. She came to the conclusion that she wasn't ready for real life, so she asked for help, which that in itself is amazing.

She is eighteen, and she doesn't know it all. Even more important she wanted us to help her. She had some of the same issues that I did growing up. Isn't it just like God to put her with someone who knows what it was like to seek men, and want to be loved? Isn't it wonderful that God would use us to help her out? God's love is…More than enough for her, just like it has been for me! You see the miracle is that he continues to use me, and my past to change the future of the girls around me, thank you, Father!

"I trust in the steadfast love of God forever and ever" (Psalms 52:8, ESV).

Watch God Work

It's neat to watch God work. However, you have to pay attention. We needed to return our movies back to Red Box. But since we didn't have the time to drive across town, I offered to drive to a convenience store to let a youth get a soda before school. Guess what was sitting right there waiting for me? Yeah, that's right, a Red Box. I smiled, and said, "Thank you, Jesus!" We were running behind, and trying to get meds for Ron.

One of the associates from campus called and said she would pick up our youth from school. God gave us plenty of time to take care of our errands. Thank you, Jesus. We pushed the envelope, trying to get things done and rushed; God wanted us to know he was working it all out. Then he got a call that Gracie our little puppy we had given away. Gracie had run away again. Now, this isn't the first time this has happened. So we just passed on the information to our friend, and just like every other time she is returned.

Gracie is then sent to the, pardon my analogy, the "DOG" house. I used to be upset when they found my puppy down the street, around the corner, in the park, or at someone else's house. God being so good has shown me that we can't worry even about the animals. He cares for them, and because he cares for them, we can relax, and just enjoy the moments that he has given us.

She doesn't belong to me, so Gracie likes to be a blessing to those around her too. Just like God allowed Gracie to bless my life. Thank you, Jesus, for the joy you bring to us each and every day. I was sitting down, and had opened a cabinet above me, God reminded me to close the door, so I wouldn't, bang my head, thank you, Jesus! I had lost my house key, again. Every time I get in a hurry I set them down, and then the hunt is on. I get so desperate, that I tell the girls if anyone finds my keys, I will give them a dollar. One girl said, "Well, you can call Mr. Ron, and he will give you his set."

Now, it's here, where I say, "They were just right here." Then one of the girls in a very questionable tone says then you shouldn't have any trouble finding them. UGH! It's then I get smart, and I asked God to help me find them. I hear the one girl say I found them, so I grabbed the dollar to pay her, and there were the keys under the dollar bill!

I opened the door, and she had two pacifiers she lost days earlier in the couch. Now she doesn't have to pay for new pacifiers, and I don't have to pay her a dollar. Thank you, Lord, that as we seek you, we find blessings.

"Ask, and it will be given to you; seek, and you will find; knock, and it will be opened to you" (Matthew 7:7, ESV).

Don't Push

Ron needed to get to the doctors for refills on his prescriptions. We didn't have the money, yeah not even for the doctor's appointment. God knew I didn't need them, because when I went in to change some information at the pharmacy. He still had two more refills, and we just got paid, so we could refill them. I also needed that $55 for the doctors to pay on my cell phone bill, which was fixing to get cut off. We took that money, and some money that was given to us by our daughter.

She just wanted to be obedient to what God told her to do. She was prompted by God to give us $100. We were able to make the cell phone bill. Probably not a BIG deal to you, but I tried and tried to get Ron to go to the doctors. You know how we women can be a little nagging at times. I probably mentioned it to him a couple of times or twenty. Whatever the reason was, he just never went. But now we know why he never had time to go to the doctor. Funny, how when things don't work out we try to push the envelope. We just end up making a mess of things. As we wait, we see God walking through, working it all out. Thank you, God, for not only helping us to pay our bills, but for finding favor with refills, so that we have enough for six months. Don't push, if it isn't working out, wait on God. He wants to bless you because, you know, that's how God rolls!

"Be strong, and let your heart take courage, all you who wait for the LORD!" (Psalms 31:24, ESV)

Dinner and a Show

Go here, go there, come back, go back, pick up this, and don't forget that; once again from the top. OMG, would this day ever end? When I was almost finished getting all the errands done, one youth called, and told me she was sick and coming home. As if I needed one more thing to alter my course. Then God had one of the ladies from another house call me, and offer to help with watching my sick youth while I pick up another youth. Then another lady calls, and asked if I could watch another youth for a couple of hours. Really is she kidding? Yes is all I can say. She then offers to pick up my third youth, which was a blessing. That way, I could get some paperwork done.

While I was trying to type the youth that I was just watching for an hour or two started up a conversation. Now, I couldn't be bothered with this child, I was doing my work. She kept talking all the while I never looked at her and never acknowledged she was even saying anything.

At this time God gets my attention, like someone knocking you on the head saying, wake up silly. I stopped turn around and begin to listen. This girl needed someone to talk to. God was giving me another opportunity to share, and pray with her. To think I almost missed an opportunity to speak your Word into a life. It was a grace-filled moment, mostly for me. Then our counselor comes over and tells me she needs an operation, please, Father God, heal her from the inside out in Jesus name. Be with the surgeon's hands, and heal her quickly; she is so special, so loved by us all; she may never even know what a blessing she has been to me. Thank you in advance for working this out in her. As if we hadn't had enough crazy stuff going on, we had to switch from minivan back to full size vans for the fifth time today.

We needed to go to a Christmas play that no one wanted to go to. Did I mention? No one! It was unanimous; there was arguing, and people being disrespectful to one another, and then we had to tell the sick girl she had to go to another cottage, misery loves company, you know! We stopped to eat at where else, McDonald's, our favorite restaurant by far... NOT!

But it got the girls quiet, and the babies had fun, so with tummies full we were off to the Christmas play. The one girl, who said her daughter, would ruin it for everyone was the one girl who enjoyed it the most! Isn't it just like that? We must have gotten lost about eleven times, because the GPS kept rerouting us at least that many times.

Rerouting didn't seem to matter, because the girls were just enjoying the ride. They were also making fun of the driver, which thank you Jesus wasn't me. Ron handled himself with class and grace as usual. Guess what I got out of this crazy day? The fact that through it all we are always given opportunities to share, we just need to be sensitive to God's hand moving, and putting everything in place so that we can. We serve such a good God.

Taming the Tongue

We got a wonderful surprise; the church that we wanted to visit tomorrow is going to be coming to the cottage to bring us a brand new TV. We always want to be grateful for what we have. Our TV was a HUGE projection screen that weighed 1000 pounds. You only could leave it in one area, if not; the angle would be hard to see. Who knows what would have been under it if we could have ever moved it. We were so excited it was a blessing; God himself ordered it! Everyone had asked if we had it on our wish list, but we never got around to it. We meant to put it on as a need for our cottage, but being so busy at Christmas, it never got done. God is so good, he did it for us.

One of our youth came in at the midnight hour, and I didn't handle myself, as I should have. I never lost my temper, but I didn't speak with tenderness, as I should have. That made it so difficult for me to go to sleep; when I finally did, it was time to get up. I could only imagine the worst. I figured the youth would be difficult and rude and anything that goes along with a know-it-all.

When she got up, she was apologetic and humble. She told me she couldn't sleep either. If I had only given it to God, so he could handle it, he would have. Forgive me, Father, for not coming to the girl in love. I came with condemnation, but you would have shown forgiveness. I think I would rather do it your way! Help me walk in your ways, so I can show them Jesus!

"Keep your tongue from evil and your lips from speaking deceit" (Psalms 34:13, ESV).

Giving Gifts

We were visiting a new church, and it was what we had been looking for the whole time. I just walked in, sat down, and I was at home. While at the church, the pastor announced that a group of bikers were coming to our cottage after church to bring us a TV. Is God's timing perfect or what? The girls got all excited and couldn't wait to come home, and move things around to make room for the new TV. When the bikers drove up there were over thirty people on bikes, and in cars, all ready to help. They got out and out POPPED a 42-inch flat screen TV with the wall mounts to put it up. Remember the HUGE TV well it took six grown men to move it out, and haul it away. The love they showed us is what made us feel so special more than getting the TV.

My goodness, we never felt so blessed to be ministered to and by so many; we had another instant family! We invited them in, and off they went to work. We shared with them stories about the girls, and they were more than willing to listen. They were touched by how God was working in their lives, and what a difference he was making. Not only did they bring this wonderful gift for us they went across the street, and hooked up a boy's cottage too! As we shared the different struggles of some of the girls, we knew we had people that wanted to add to these youth's lives. The kids were so excited and so blown away. One of the youth just sat there looking at everyone amazed that people would be so kind.

I wondered if they knew they were being the hands and feet of Jesus. They made the kids feel special, and even allowed them to take pictures on the motorcycles. As they were getting ready to leave they all bowed their heads and prayed over the house, campus, youth, and the workers of the cottages. They said we heard you have some carpenter needs. I showed them some of the things we needed fixed. They said we will be sending someone over to fix doors and anything else you might need this week.

We have doors that are holding on by a thread, toilets that rock like a rocker, drawers that won't slide out, and chairs that are falling apart. The cottage is wonderful, but when you put eight kids into one-cottage things are going to get broke and do. When the carpenter came back the next day, he spent several days on our cottage. The time was over, a hundred hours, all at someone else's expense. OMG! When these people mean they wanted to be a blessing, they weren't kidding. I'm a speechless, overwhelmed, and holding back tears. God is so good, we are so loved, and yet he continues to show us more.

Later that evening I got to share the gospel with a youth that was visiting. She realized that she didn't deserve it but more than anything she wanted to know she had a father that would always be there for her. She bowed her head, prayed and invited Jesus into her heart and life, OMG! This has been a day so remarkable and truly ordered by God. Thank you, Father for allowing me to be a part of your wonderful plan. So many gifts are all given because of you!

"How much more will your Father who is in heaven give good things to those who ask him!" (Matthew 7:11b, ESV)

Words Worth Remembering

One night, we got to hear a wonderful testimony from an associate during staff meeting, and it never ceased to amaze me the journeys people go through to finally get to Jesus. It is definitely a journey that we should figure out quicker. Somehow we don't, and we have to take the long route to get there. Sometimes I think about the children of Israel and how they wandered for longer than they should have because they just didn't get it.

I got to pick up a young man that was helping with the play we were putting on at the campus. While he was in the car with us I shared with him—one more opportunity to plant a seed. I lost my phone and found out that I left it at the hospital, so Ron went back to get it. Thank you, Jesus, we found it again. Silly phone—it just likes to take off and do its own thing!

After dinner we got an opportunity to do a faith walk around the campus for the Christmas pageant they put on every year. Wow, what a wonderful way to share Jesus. As we all took our place at each scene and prayed for God to be glorified in everything that was done. One of our youth got up and with all of her heart she prayed so eloquently that we were all speechless. Thank you, Father, for allowing us to be there at that moment to witness God at work in this young lady's life. Not to mention the blessing we received from just hearing it.

We may be able to pray and truly be sincere. To say all the right things but to be touched so deeply is incredible, and to think she almost bowed out. Thank you, Jesus, for all the change we are seeing in her life and the difference she is making in ours.

"Therefore, if anyone is in Christ, he is a new creation. The old has passed away; behold, the new has come" (2 Corinthians 5:17, esv).

Clean I Mean

What a blessing. We went to the donation bay on campus and there was a brand NEW washer and dryer. Ours have been on their last legs for a while now; the reason I know is because every time we do laundry they take legs and walk. Seriously the washer will start out in one spot, and end up in another. I know its legs have got to be tired, so we now get to give them a rest. Thank you, Jesus! I thank God, because we have so many people that give so graciously. They could just have sold those machines; they weren't even a year old, instead they chose to bless the campus with them.

Here is a neat thing, our washer had just quit working the night before, but we didn't know it. It was only when we got up the next morning that we saw the washer was full of water and wouldn't drain. Talk about timing.

God always sees what we need, and working it out beforehand. Thank you, God, for allowing things to last longer than they are supposed to. For allowing us to be clean on the inside and out.

"The fear of the LORD is clean, enduring forever; the rules of the LORD are true, and righteous all together" (Psalms 19:9, ESV).

Service of Sacrifice

We were up at the crack of dawn and on the road at 7:15 a.m.! We were visiting another church. It was a small church that had always given to the campus, and we had been invited to stay for lunch. They put on a play for Christmas, and they did a great job with it. Then we got a chance to see people giving from their need, which choked me up. I had never been a part of something like that, and it was very humbling to see a church respond so graciously to people they had never even met.

Thank you, Jesus; now I see what you meant about the widow's mite. After the play our director Gary spoke; Ron and another youth also spoke about how God moves on campus. The youth spoke about how blessed she was to have gotten an opportunity to be at the children's home, and how we had been making such a difference in her life. But she mostly spoke about what God had been doing in her life, and all the changes he had made in her. It even touched the girls that were very distant.

Wow! To see the girls touched where they were; that was sweet. I was so very proud of all the things I got to witness, and somehow would still not see all the wonderful blessings God was working out. As we were leaving a gentleman told us that he lost his wife a year ago and asked that there be NO flowers just send the money to the children's home.

Wow! To think people think of us even when we aren't aware; it choked me up again. Then after lunch, which was so yummy, a gentleman came up to me and gave me a check for the campus. I was grateful that I was a part of something bigger than I could even imagine. We got home and got ready for the last night of the pageant and it really was a hit. So many showed up, but only God knows the changes it will make in people's lives. That's where faith comes in. We plant hundreds of seeds that God will continue to grow. More than anything we pray God receives all the glory for all our efforts! Thank you God for showing up and letting us receive!

Bethany's Blessing

Bethany was seventeen when I came to campus. She had lived through more at seventeen than most people live their whole lives. She ended up at our campus because of her circumstances at home. Bethany's mom died when she was fourteen, so she was forced to live with her dad and step-mom. The first time she went to stay with her dad she was twelve, and she ended up being there until she was sixteen. Her dad and stepmom abused her in every way possible for four years. They even ended up in jail when it was all said and done. She came to campus because at sixteen she had gotten pregnant.

She said she was looking to be loved and accepted and ended up with a child. When she came to campus, she already had Valery. Valery was a preemie, four pounds and two ounces and was always behind the curve when it came to her health. Bethany had a lot of anger issues, and she didn't care who she cussed out, including me.

When I met her, she annoyed me by the way she would ignore her daughter. Unless someone came around then she would pick her up and play with her. Mostly the baby was getting all the attention, and she wanted attention too. I would tell her she needed to watch Valery closely, or clean up after her, and even needed to pick her up when she was fixing to get hurt.

When we would have to correct what she was doing, she would go off. I never understood why she could go off at a moment's notice. As Bethany talked to other youth on campus, they shared what was the change in their lives. She talked to several houseparent's as well. Everyone was more than willing to share what God had done in his or her lives.

It was hard to believe that someone could love her with all that she had been through. She told me that she had never felt loved or accepted until she came to the campus. On July 28, 2010, she went into her room prayed and asked Jesus to forgive her and come into her heart. She wanted to have the same kind of love everyone else talked about. From the moment she prayed, her life began to change.

Now I would like to say her life changed dramatically, but it was a slow transformation. She would apologize after she messed up, which was nothing like before. She was still having trouble taking care of her baby though. Valery had a lot of health issues, which made it even more difficult for Bethany to handle. She admitted that she wasn't ready to be a mother, but she was still selfish. She didn't want to be the first one on campus to give her child up. The baby wasn't growing like she was supposed to. She was struggling with crawling and walking but she did get there.

One night while she was in her room God began to talk to her about giving up her baby for adoption. She didn't listen and continued to ignore God's drawing. Several months went by, and she was having a hard time keeping Valery clean and even started resenting her. This still didn't change her mind. One night she fought with God while she had gone to bed. God told her she needed to give her baby up. It didn't make her a bad parent. It would let everyone know she loved her baby enough to give her a better life.

She would tell God, "No", and then say, "Why me? Why do I have to do this? Everyone will think I'm a bad parent if I give her up. They won't let me stay here if I don't have a baby. My baby will hate me. How can I live without her? Does this mean I can't see her anymore? Who will become her parents? I can't do it, it's too hard."

That's when God said to her "Trust in the Lord with all your heart. Lean not on your own understanding. In all your ways acknowledge him; and he will make your paths straight."

At that point she stopped fighting and went to sleep. The next day at church she walked into church and the first thing she saw was a HUGE billboard sign that said Trust in the Lord with all your heart. Lean not on your own understanding. In all your ways acknowledge him; and he will make your paths straight. She cried because she knew God was dealing with her and she finally said, "Okay, I will do it." She went home and told her houseparent's that she was ready to put her baby's needs before her selfishness. She found out that a couple at the church was looking to adopt a child. So they met for breakfast and began to talk to her.

Now Valery was very standoffish and wouldn't' go to anyone. The first time the lady met little Valery, she grabbed her little finger and went walking around the store. Another confirmation for Bethany, she couldn't believe it. Valery never went to anyone. Peace fell on her as she watched Valery interact with her new mother. Finally, a place where she could feel she belonged.

God wasn't through with them yet. Bethany did an open adoption so she could stay close to Valery and be a part of her life. The couple was wonderful and in awe that God would send them this amazing little girl. After six months, Valery is finally on the growth chart for her age, which she never was before. Happy, healthy, and loved—what more could you ask for a child except for a wonderful example of a loving mother that thought more about her child, than she did about herself.

Thank you, God for using what could have been the worse of circumstances and pouring out your love to everyone involved. Bethany not only made two choices that affected her life, but she is now going to college studying to be a nurse. She wants to help others through the healing process, who better than one that needed healing.

"Trust in the LORD with all your heart, and do not lean on your own understanding" (Proverbs 3:5, ESV).

Language of Love

It is so wonderful when your children teach you something. I wasn't feeling particularly good and Ron was going out to get something to eat. Modern conveniences these days are a blessing and a curse. We love to eat out, so we eat more than we should. Doesn't home-cooked food taste better anyway? I will get off my soapbox. When Ron brought the food back it was completely wrong. So I started to complain, my son was standing there and said "Mom, just say thank you".

Wow, he was so right in the midst of trying to please me, because someone else messed up the order, I was going to be fussy. But he reminded me to be grateful for what had just been done for me. I thanked Ron for the effort, and even choked down some of it. My eyes were opened to a terrible habit I needed to break.

How quick are we to fuss when someone, even God doesn't get it right; at least the perception of what we think is right, and we are quick to snap.

Father forgive me for not being grateful to my husband, family, friends, and especially you when all they are trying to do is help. Thank you for such a wonderful husband that only wants to please me. Thank you for my son, who gave me that gentle reminder. Thank you, God, for always showing me I'm not too old to change that my words should only reflect love.

"Above all, keep loving one another earnestly, since love covers a multitude of sins" (1 Peter 4:8, ESV).

Sharing Self

I got up late, and I didn't go to church. I did share devotion with a youth in the house. I shared with her how God wanted to bless her. I began to share with her how we are supposed to give to God the first fruits of your labor. As we talked, I showed her several times how God has blessed me when I put him first. She didn't know how it all worked, and it didn't make sense to her.

You would only have $50. Tithe $40 and you still will be able to pay your bills of $120. That's when I told her that she has to start trusting sometime. We walked by faith (believing in something you cannot see) and not by sight. I told her I trust God with everything, and he has never let me down. Later on that day the youth put back $21 to give at church. When we got to church she was smiling from ear to ear as she gave. It did my heart good to see her start to get the principles of giving.

You see it was very difficult for someone like her to give since she holds on tight to everything she gets. She hardly even shares because she has done without for most of her life. Thank you, God for allowing her to look beyond her circumstances to honor you with her first fruits. She is learning early that she will reap a harvest she doesn't even know she is planted, thank you.

"Give, and it will be given to you. Good measure, pressed down, shaken together, running over, will be put into your lap. For with the measure you use it will be measured back to you" (Luke 6:38, ESV).

Come on In

What a crazy day! We managed to get all the girls and their babies to the doctors. It seems as though they will all live. After the appointment we all went to a movie, and had a great time. Then we went to a birthday lunch. Did I mention cake? Every time there is cake being served we need to be a part of that. We just have to sample it to make sure it will be okay for everyone else. It's what we do, we are kind that way.

I did a few more errands, and then it was home. We had our friends come over from out of town. We told them just to help themselves, and let themselves in. When we got there they had invited other people as well. We didn't mind because it was really the only place that they could stretch out, and get comfortable. They ate, played games, and visited for hours. Ron and I thought it was cool. What a blessing that people feel so comfortable that they just come right on in, and make themselves at home. That's a ministry in itself. Jesus talked about it—if they welcome you, stay, and if they don't shake the dust off of your feet as if you never knew them.

I heard the comment made that they never felt so at peace in a place as ours; thank you, Jesus, because everything we have is yours. Every place we lay our head down is an opportunity to welcome others in. I guess I never realized the importance of making others feel welcomed. It's because we're sharing Jesus. It's exactly what Jesus would have done; thank you, Jesus, for giving us this opportunity.

Roadblocks

We work with a young lady, who is as sweet as she can be, when she isn't at work. She will give you the shirt off of your back. So now you're saying but? When she comes to work we immediately need to drop what we are doing, and we make sure we do everything she wants. On this particular day she comes in, and she tells Ron and me that we need to talk. We are sure there is something we need to fix because that's usually what people do when they say we need to talk.

She starts off by saying that she was fixing to go on a mission trip. She told us, she has made all the arrangements to get there and for the return trip, but she isn't comfortable about it.

Now I get it she isn't talking about work. She is talking about ministry outside of work.

It seems that as though every time she jumps through one hoop in order to go, another door shuts.

As more mature Christians, we listened, and allowed God to show us things.

She then said that the travel arrangements kept getting changed. That she was supposed to go with one group, and now she wouldn't even be going with them. They can, however, guarantee when she will be coming back. She was worried about not being able to be back on time. That's what she wanted to work out arrangements for when she would be off. She asked if we would cover for her if it took longer for her to get back. It's then that we prayed with her. Then we told her God wouldn't make it hard for you to do this mission trip. You would just need to really investigate everything before you go. I thought that this didn't sound right.

A few days later, she came back, and she was shaking. I asked her what's wrong. She told us all the sordid details of this mission trip. When it's all said and done, it was a scam to buy, and sell people.

I said, "You serious?"

As she talked she told us that God was making it difficult for her because he knew what she was getting into. She then said, "To think if I hadn't come to talk to you, and get your insight I might have gone. You would have never seen me again."

We reminded her that God would make things easy. It's us that keep trying and trying even though doors are slammed shut. Thank you, God that at every turn you put a roadblock in front of her. Even when she wanted to drive through them, there was another one to slow her down. Thank you, God, for all the signs, that lead us straight to you, please help us to read them.

Your Blessings MAT-ter

I only went out for a minute, but I sure received a blessing when I did. I went to the office, and they had a check for me, thank you, Jesus! Then as I was leaving the building I noticed a plastic mat, you know the kind that goes under your computer chair so you can move around on the carpet easily. This was a perfectly good mat, and it was just lying there. Since I needed one I grabbed it up and said what else but, "thank you, Jesus".

The office said they were throwing them away, so I took it as a gift, and Ron was excited to have it. Now, you may think that's no big deal, but do you see all the wonderful ways God continues to bless us daily?

If we weren't truly thankful for everything, why in the world would he want to give us anything else? Your Father knows what you need, and is more than happy to get it for you. But here's the kicker—be patient, not only will he get it for you, but it won't cost you a dime.

You see when we came to work here they told us we wouldn't get rich. But they were wrong, we are so rich in so many ways, it's just fun watching everything unfold. Thank you, Jesus, for all of your blessings because every one of them Mat-ter. (Did you like that play on words?)

"Blessed are the people to whom such blessings fall! Blessed are the people whose God is the LORD!" (Psalms 144:15, ESV)

All This and Heaven Too

As I reflect on the past year, I have so much to be thankful for. Many came to know Jesus as their personal savior—a dozen to be exact. Not to mention how many we got to witness to, and plant seeds into their young lives. Thank you, Jesus, for allowing us to be used to see so many lives changed because of your Grace and Mercy.

We saw an eighty-year-old come to the Lord as well as teenagers. It will be so incredible to watch what God will do with all of their lives. Next, we saw God close the door on one job and open another. What an incredible time we had as we watched God put everything into place. We were so blessed that we got paid during a transition time. The checks never ran out.

As we waited for two months for the paperwork to go through, God provided. We called about a position for houseparent's, and the job wasn't even posted yet, a God thing to be sure. We got interviewed, and the next day the job was ours. We gave up all of our furniture because God told us to. We sold it all for $3,200; then when we got to our new place, we had no furniture so we furnished our entire house for $355. A couch, chair, two beds, a table and four chairs, a refrigerator, a microwave, a bookshelf, a TV stand, a dresser and there was more. Do you get the idea?

Next, to watch people's lives be transformed, because they get God is just incredible. We are finally in a church that we feel like we are home, and you know how special that can be.

We had a wonderful dinner, which Ron fixes every year; to celebrate how good God has been to us. The feast includes steak, lobster, snow crab, and all the fixings. We have so much, and yet it's so special to bring the New Year in praying and giving thanks. I texted most of my friends and family to bring in the New Year, and then as I was receiving some well wishes back. I heard a knock on the door—the girls left us a handmade New Year's card.

Looking back we have God pouring his love out on us including our family, friends, and the staff around us, that helps make our lives so special. We are truly blessed! This year promises to be filled with love, joy, peace, hope, and excitement because God is continually at work. It's exciting to watch him move. Thank you, God, for all of this and heaven too, as my grandma would say!

Blue Baby

As I drove everyone to their respective places, I was off to find hats for our weekend murder mystery. Leaving the seventh store with no luck, I finally asked God to help me find our fun hats. Would you believe it? I drove two blocks, and there it was a clothing store, but more important…hats and more hats, every kind, every color, and every style…thank you, Jesus. My next mission if I choose to accept it—table and chairs for the cottage, a new one, since ours was about the turn of the century.

After looking in several stores without any success, I looked to the left and there was a furniture store I hadn't noticed before. Imagine the table I had been looking for was there, and it was $500 cheaper than I intended to pay.

We went to the YMCA where we swam, and enjoyed playing with the girls. We had one of the babies in the water. We kind of figured when her lips and hands turned blue that it was time for her to get out. So we wrapped her in swaddling towels and laid her in the cement—not the perfect picture you're painting, I supposed.

We got out and took the baby into the showers to get her warm, and let her wash off a little. Herein lies the problem; the towel was soaked from us leaving her by the pools edge where water was splashing her.

One of the girls offered her brand new towel with monogram letters to wrap her in. After she had taken a warm shower, and I was changing when I heard OMG she wet all over my new towel. I laughed hysterically. The baby was so comfortable that she finally relaxed and let it go, go, and go. We decided after that that it might not have been such a good thing to swim when there was snow outside, but life is an adventure and we sure know how to live it. When we got home, we put the babies to bed and went to parenting classes, as if our day wasn't busy enough.

The girls were worn out, but the highlight was when one of the girls came up to me and said, "Hey I didn't get to do my devotion today. Can we do it now?"

Wow, these are the moments that blow me away. We did our devotion together and share our thoughts about it, which was always very insightful. She is taking it to heart. We see it when she says prayers for others. Just a week ago she couldn't stand this person, and now God was working that out in her. What an amazing God we serve. Thank you, God, for another typical day in the life of your servant.

Patience in the Process

This day began like the usual with more errands than minutes in the day. I ended up having to take one youth to her doctor's appointment. While we were at the doctors, they also looked at her son. He was sick, so we killed two birds with one stone. Then as I was coming home, I found out that one of our youth was causing havoc with Ron. All he was supposed to do was pick this youth up from school, then her baby, and come back. He had the wrong car seat so he had to return to get a different one.

When Ron came back with a different one, she refused to use it as well. Here is where the cursing and yelling came in. Now, don't get me wrong she was cussing the whole time, but by now she was hitting her fist into the van. After fifteen minutes they finally got the right one. You see we only live less than five minutes away, so she was being overly dramatic.

She ended up in the office, and was asked if she could handle herself the rest of the night. She said, yes but she meant NO! She got in the van and cussed out two more girls and then me. Was she on a roll or what? Then we got back to the house, and she decided that she wasn't going to do anything she was asked to do. After dinner she was reminded that her laundry had to be done by 9:00 p.m., she got mad and left everything a mess.

Now this is not a typical day, but lately she is making this a routine. We have to ask ourselves why we do this, because it is right where God wants us. All these girls come with baggage, and as long as they live in there past they are defeated. I get a chance to talk to her, and remind her that God loves her. She is more than her past; God has a plan for good, a plan for hope. She needs to remember that everyone might not have the best childhood, but God never promised the road would be easy, but that he would see you through. I reminded her that she needs to be the example she wants to see in her kids.

Now don't get me wrong I wasn't done with this girl. I was pretty much sick of all her nonsense. I was ready to kick her to the curb, but God reminded me that he hasn't quit on me, and I wasn't going to quit on her. I want to, everything in me says she will never change, but then I'm reminded that my whole life is a process and God is so patient to see me through. How in the world can I throw in the towel if God hasn't? Father thanks for always being patient with my work in process, and I won't be finished until I'm home.

"But if we hope for what we do not see, we wait for it with patience" (Romans 8:25, ESV).

Less Is More

It's a new day but the same game—more of the same from our friendly youth is progress. She was given a request and refused to comply. In our cottage, most everyone knows you take turns with everything including the seats in the van. If you were in front, you move to the middle, and then to the back. Well our work in process has an excuse for every time it's her turn to be in the back. Let's just say she is the skinniest, and she could get to the back a lot easier. She hasn't figured out how to be kind to others yet.

This day she decides she is going to take the place where our pregnant girl is sitting. When asked to move she quickly she replies it's just a seat, so I sit there for a minute. God shows me something real easy rather than make everyone else late I put it in drive and go. As I drive, I tell our work in process that as long as she continues to take others' seat, she will be sitting in the back for thirty days from the time she gets it right. I leave it alone, and let her think on it. Funny how we think we get these wonderful ideas when all long it's God, and we take the credit. Forgive me, Father, everything comes from you—all glory and honor belongs to you. It was a stroke of genius because she had nothing to say. Whew what a blessing.

As we get back to the cottage, she has to get ready to walk over to another cottage. The roads are icy, so we do not know how long it's going to take to get to Tulsa and back. Now let me tell you it's only fifty yards to the house, but she looks at me and says, "If I get sick I'm blaming it on you." I said, "okay."

Remember how we could walk everywhere for hours and thought nothing of it. These days the kids struggle to walk a block, no kidding. Barely have I got back from one task, when I get a call saying go pick up the "work in process" baby. He was sick and couldn't stay in the daycare.

So off I went, and then I dropped him off at our child development center. Then I called in his doctor for an appointment. After school we picked everyone up, and I took them to the office. Our assistant director wanted words with this youth. I thank you Jesus that she has such kind words to say to her because I was ready to drop a bomb on her. God showed me to listen, so I did. Right before my eyes this young lady transformed. The love came back and the anger left. It was such a God moment. All I remember was letting her know how much we loved her, and how awesome we thought she was doing.

Ron spoke to her, and he did an amazing job, and so did our director. By the time we left everyone was hugging…thank you, Jesus, for showing up, and showing out we would still be dealing with a very unruly youth. Instead, she accepts her consequences and humbled herself with even serving others in the cottage.

We went to the YMCA, and she didn't get to go, but still she had a wonderful attitude. Lord, you blow me away when we allow you to say what we in the flesh wouldn't. We speak life and that's exactly what you do, thank you.

"Do not be conformed to this world, but be transformed by the renewal of your mind, that by testing you may discern what is the will of God, what is good and acceptable and perfect" (Romans 12:2, ESV).

Clayton Knows Love

We got into Austin at our daughter's house at about 9:00 p.m. We were hanging out watching TV just unwinding when my daughter called me into the bedroom. There was nothing unusual about her wanting to talk, so as I stepped into her room he was sitting up on the bed shaking and crying. I asked her what was wrong.

She said, I couldn't do this anymore. I asked her again what was wrong. She told me that her friend Clayton was just in their and that he talked about killing himself.

She said, he took a lot of pills, drank a lot of alcohol, and just cut himself and that there was a knife under the bed that he just used. I asked where is he now? She said he just left and is walking outside.

I told her this is a cry for help sweetie. I stepped out of the room and told Ron that he needed to go talk to this young man that was trying to hurt himself. Ron quickly got on his shoes and headed out the door. I went back in and proceeded to talk to our daughter and find out anything else we might need to know.

She said he is bleeding and had been banging his head against the wall. I grabbed some shoes and hurried out the door to help find him. I walked down the alleyway and found him and Ron sitting down in a wooded area. I asked if he was okay.

Ron said we are talking. I then asked Clayton are you okay?

He said, "I'm tired of this stuff. I have tried talking to God, praying, everything, it's not working."

I said, "Do you know how much you are loved?"

He said "whatever, I just don't see it, and I am not doing this anymore."

"Well you're not a quitter. You race and sometimes you fall off. Sometimes you don't win, but you never quit. You're a champion, and you want to win! You keep trying because you want the prize at the end.

"You haven't even begun this walk with God, but I know you, and you want to be the *best* and you keep trying until you get there," I told him.

I walked away after that because I knew that Ron needed some time with him. I went back to talk to Michelle. She was very worried, upset, and completely wiped out from what had just happened. As we talked I reminded Michelle that this was not her fault. Clayton had a bad week and month.

I found out that he had just been issued a divorce degree from his last marriage. He got fired unjustly from his job, got in a fight with his brothers, been turned down for unemployment, and his wife was trying to take the only vehicle he owned.

On top of that when he tried to talk to someone about his problems no one even cared enough to listen. Not even his mom because it seems as though she had problems of her own and didn't need any more drama. As she continued to talk me, without even thinking, I started praying.

My daughter grabbed my hand and we prayed that God would send his ministering angels to watch over him and her. We rebuked any evil spirit that was trying to attack his thoughts that would make him feel like he had nowhere to turn to but death. We asked God to open his heart and to allow salvation to come to him. As I prayed there was a perfect peace that poured out over the place. I knew this was his moment, he was going to accept Jesus as his savior, and all I could do was smile.

I explained to Michelle that God walks quietly by in our lives orchestrating events to draw people to himself. We only need to be sensitive to what he is doing, because he loves us so much. He put things in place for our benefit. So we sat there just talking and waiting to watch God move. Wow, Ron and the young man came back, Ron walked into the room and told us to stay put. Then he said could we pray, so we bowed our heads and prayed. The spirit was heavy in the room. I wished you could have been there. He was going to clean up then finish talking to him. They went into the living room and talked. Ron told him a lot of things, but it wasn't until he heard him say you are worthy of being loved that he broke down.

He cried so deeply and so hard that he finally had room for God. You see when you got nothing left that's when God can come in to fill you to overflowing. He bowed his head and prayed for the first time in his thirty-seven years of life and asked God to forgive him, and come into his heart. I could see it all over him. This peace that just washes over you—the years of fighting, hurt, and emptiness was gone.

He finally got it; God loved him so much that he took the time to create him. While he was living on the streets at twelve years old, he never knew how much he was valued. You see with no fault of his own, his mom and dad were nonexistent. When at the age of eleven, his dad would tell him here is a fishing pole, if you don't catch anything you don't eat. He would not only have to walk three miles away, but when he did catch anything, he would have to cook it.

He found out he was allergic to shellfish because he caught a whole bunch of them. Then he ate them and doubled over in pain. When he woke up, he was all by himself and there was vomit everywhere. His life was so dark—no food, no home, no one to love him. He figured he would be better on his own, so at twelve years old that's what he did.

God watched over him all this time to bring him to this place, so that he finally was home. So ask yourself this question, as God walked through, what unfolded? We just happened to be right where God wanted us, and one very dark night, one young man came to the end of his rope and met Jesus, and his life will never be the same.

Oh and here's one more thing it was the National Day of Prayer, it was midnight when we started praying for salvation for this one young man. You think prayer works, well, our lives testify to it every day. It was God walking quietly through Clayton's life to reach him, to let him know he was loved, he had value, and he now has a Father that he knows will be there for him.

Now, Clayton's walk won't be like mine, but then he will reach people I never could. Clayton smiles now, hug now, and loves now because he knows now that God cares. Isn't that what we all want? Thank you, Father, for Clayton's new life that's full of love, joy, and acceptance that only comes from you! Thank you for sharing your heart with people that truly needed a touch!

"For God so loved the world, that he gave his only Son, that whoever believes in him should not perish but have eternal life. For God, did not send his Son into the world to condemn the world; but in order that the world might be saved through him" (John 3: 16–17, ESV).

Don't Stop Trying

While at a friend's house we had been talking how we need to stay in touch. It's always easier said than done these days. She talked about how she would call, and talk to her dad if only he would call and talk to her. I then asked her how she was doing with this tit for tat stuff.

She asked what I meant. I said you never know what good you will do speaking to your dad. For example, he doesn't have the confidence because he doesn't have the support from his family. Hearing from you can make him feel loved and valued that maybe only you can give him.

I said I had the opportunity to stay in contact with my dad, but because he wouldn't call me I didn't call him. Now how silly is that? I would call him one time to see how he was doing, and because he didn't call me back I figured he didn't care. I tried several times, but then I quit. Nows here's what you need to know, Suppose if I had kept calling, I might have begun a relationship with him that could have grown into something special. I might have gotten an opportunity to share Jesus with him, but I never did.

I missed the chance to share with him all because I was waiting for him to call first. I later found out that he couldn't call because he was in a fixed income, and he couldn't pay a large phone bill because all he had was a landline.

I told my friend that if you're waiting for your dad to call you first, you're wrong. You need to take every opportunity to be a part of the family that God gave you. When you call it makes a difference for them. Thank you, Lord for opening my eyes to help someone else who was going down the same road I did. Thank you, God, for letting us reach out and affect the lives of so many—one person at a time.

Really Ready

Everyone was up and ready then to their usual places, and then on to our annual training for the year. Believe me, there is a lot of training that goes into working with kids. Our boss tries to make it as fun as she can. We learn a lot, and we always need a refresher course. I had barely sat down for a few minutes when I got three phones calls.

I disregarded them, but they were persistent, so I answered the phone. It's a girl calling in to say she was going into labor. I jumped into my van. I went to Tulsa to pick her up and take her to the hospital. We got there, and the valet took our car to park it. The cool thing was there was no guessing where I was going to have to park. It's just one less thing I had to worry about. Then they checked her in, told her she would need to get undressed and put on her robe.

What did she do? She put a gown over her clothes. Like I haven't seen girl parts before…really? I told her she was going to need to take them off. She went into the bathroom, and when she came out she had her shorts and bra on.

She said that she couldn't do that and they would just have to work with this. Really, I think how did you get pregnant? The doctors came in and asked her to remove her undergarments. At that point, she slipped the bottoms off. They examined her and right back went on the shorts. They told her that they would have to examine her again. She said I will take them off then…crazy girl but what are you going to do?

She went to sleep during the contractions. Guess she figured it was better to try and sleep. The next time they came in to check her, they released her to go home. The staff told her what to look for, so we were off again. I went back to the training classes, and took her to the office, so they could monitor her. When we picked everyone up it was dinnertime. No one felt like cooking, so it was easier to do a drive by. While at the restaurant one baby, for whatever reason, decided to whine. I talked to the little guy, since the mom couldn't handle it. After our talk he sat down, calm, and ready to eat…thank you, Jesus. After that we went home and played a game, just to get the girls to unwind. Now, I know God was trying to teach me something through all of this. For example: He is in control when no one else is. I'm happy he is, I don't want his job. He is much better with it…thank you, Father, for being our help, even when we don't realize it.

Richly Blessed by Ron

After lunch with the kids we went to the town of Guthrie where we would be staying the night at a haunted mansion. It's not like I believe in ghost, just the Holy Ghost. Anyway, it was a murder mystery "whodunit" dinner and solve the mystery. It has all the charm and ambience that a haunted mansion would have. We all dressed up for the part (1920) and when the time was right, we gave certain clues to the mystery. All in all it was a blast, we laughed so hard and enjoyed every minute.

Then as we were finished with the mystery, we went to bed. I remember saying in Jesus name you have no place here so you have to leave. You see they have heard stories that spirits haunted the place. You know the funny thing is we told the owner we could anoint the house and pray the spirits out of there.

She said no way leave it like you found it. Ron had already spoken it. The sad thing was if she welcomed them back it would be worse than before. It was just like when Jesus drove the demons out, and unless God filled the house, they would come back stronger and even more than before. I just watched and saw how people give into all the nonsense and refused to believe the truth instead of the lies.

Father, thank you for being the truth in a world full of darkness; open their eyes that they may see the truth. Breakfast was once again fun as the owner told us about the mansion, and how she came to be a part of the history of the house. The stories were neat to hear and just added to the experience. We left and the kid gave me a giant cookie cake, I thoroughly enjoyed it and shared it with everyone.

We took the scenic route home and enjoyed the drive. God, you are so good. You laid the foundations of the world, and yet you took the time to paint us a beautiful picture. May I never get tired of seeing your handiwork?

We got home safely and then Ron goes and gets us some fun movies to watch; it was very enjoyable. Through all of this weekend God showed me several things. First, I married an incredible man. He played his part beautifully, and then made everyone have fun in the process.

Second, I realized even though he was told to sit by other people I knew he loved me. I never got that before because I was selfish, and I thought that if he wasn't paying 100 percent attention to me, he didn't love me.

Third, God showed me that the more I allow Ron to minister to others and do what God has called him to do, the more time he will have for me. It was the first time that Ron carried on a conversation with someone else; even though I was right there he knew the men needed some attention so he gave it to them.

Fourth, God gave me the man of my dreams because he is totally sold out to God, which means he knows how to love me. I get it, thank you, Father, for this wonderful man I get to share this time and space with. I am blessed and in awe that you would share him with me. Thank you, Father.

Love so Overwhelming

I'm fifty today, not that I feel any different but I sure have been treated special by my husband and kids and even friends and family. I must have received about thirty calls, and everyone was wishing me well on my birthday. Then at about 8:00 a.m., I got a ring on my doorbell telling me that one of my youths was going into labor, and she wanted me to drive her, but I let our associate handle it. It's what God wanted me to do. It was something about allowing those two to get closer. She had it at 1:30 a.m., a girl and she was very happy.

Now I have another birthday buddy, fifty years apart. Here is something interesting. I have an aunt, brother, and nephew all born on my birthday. My dad had a sister, daughter, son, and grandson all born on the same day. I wonder what the odds of that happening are. If you figure it out let me know.

Then Ron gave me a wonderful birthday card, cake, and crosses—what a surprise. He blew me away even though he doesn't know it I will cherish this birthday forever, because he truly thought of me! We again just took it easy. There was a lot to be said for actually resting on your day off.

Then out of the blue a friend of mine spoke a prophetic word over me, it gave me such peace. Here's what it said: The Lord says, "My daughter, you are so blessed, for you have my favor, and my eye is upon you. You have the gift of joy (healing to the soul) and gratitude and are like the seeder going to and fro spreading my seed where you may go. Do not worry my daughter because I know your needs, and I see your deeds. You have my attention, and I am about to produce a great harvest for you. For the farmer, who plants a field of corn, does he not expect and bring in farmhands to assist with the harvest? I am sending you a helper, and you will bring them joy (healing) as they work alongside of you. I love you my daughter, and I will be your provision. You are blessed because I say so, and my words do not return void. I love you, Brenda."

Now if that doesn't make you feel special you must be dead. Thank you, Lord, for speaking life into me this weekend, I will never be the same.

Encourage Others Even Now

It was great to sleep late. I got to sleep in, and it was good since my cold has kept me up all night. Then I got a call from a friend who was in Austin. She has really gone through some tough times the past few years. It began with a motorcycle accident that left her paralyzed from the waist down. Her husband then divorced her leaving her to fend for herself. She has been in over eight different facilities in the past three years. Now, she is in a nursing home/rehab center. She was physically, emotionally, and spiritually drained. After she told me that she doesn't pray anymore because she has nothing to say God, God told me to tell her to write.

He didn't say what to write, so I gave her some ideas. She listened and after encouraging her I got an opportunity to pray with her. Then I told her I would call her back that evening and see how she was doing and pray with her again. I told her I was going to stand in the gap until she was ready to take over.

I got to talk to a pastor friend of ours and was reminded that we have been a blessing to her even when she didn't believe. Now she is taking steps of faith to show God she is serious about trusting him with every fiber of her life. This is quite a journey for her because she hasn't had a lot of people encouraging her.

Thank you, Lord, for her taking steps toward you. Now you can do even more in her life. Then later on that evening I called her back to pray with her. We only have our word if we lose that we have nothing. She didn't answer, so I called two other times. I decided to pray with her by leaving a message, so that's just what I did. Thank you, Jesus for allowing me to be obedient, so that I can be used by you.

"Therefore encourage one another and build one another up, just as you are doing" (1 Thessalonians 5:11, ESV).

Consumed by Christ

Got a call from my friend in Austin who told me she received my message on her messaging machine, and listened to the prayer, and was blessed by it. She was blessed so much that she revealed to me that she got out of bed, got dressed, and decided to write. To my surprise, it was nothing like I thought it would be. It was about how she came to know God as her personal savior.

Thank you, Jesus, in your word. It says restore to me the joy of my salvation, and that's just what you did…what a transformation! She wrote a page and a half, and she asked if she could read it to me. The words blew me away about how she came to accept Jesus Christ, and isn't that the greatest story of all.

So I prayed with her again, reminding her of God's word, and how we are to rejoice. This is the day that you have made, and we will rejoice and be glad in it. Everyday is an opportunity to get it right. We talked and just that quick God was renewing her mind. She had purpose and was willing to try. I called her after dinner and asked her how her day was. She was very busy helping the ladies around the nursing home. What a blessing to be able to step out of the way and help others. She even asked the ladies if she could bless the meal…wow, just the day before she didn't have a prayer left in her and, now, amazing.

She said it was a good day and told me about the different people she has a chance to minister to. You see sometimes we need to help others, so that we aren't consumed by ourselves. God once again gave her hope…it's amazing how you work, Father, so subtle and yet so glorious, thank you!

Snowed in and everything cancelled—God is allowing me to get rest to get over this never ending cold. It was a nice day even though I felt like crud. We took naps, and rested, ahh, naps, they are not overrated. Then later that evening I talked to my friend once again, we must have talked for an hour and a half.

We had to; God was working something out in her. At first, she was very hurt at how everyone had let her down. But by the time we were finished, she realized that we were all human and we made mistakes. Only God has the monopoly on perfect.

I told her that until she puts her trust in God and not man, they would let her down every time. I told her until God is all you will need; you are always going to be in need. There was some healing taking place, and she was receiving the words…thank you, Jesus, for being the only difference.

"This is the day that the LORD has made; let us rejoice and be glad in it" (Psalms 118:24, ESV).

Mimic the Master

We went shopping with the girls for summer clothes. They actually started taking pride in the way they looked, when you took the time to show them how nice they could look. The sad thing about these girls was that no one ever told them how special they were, and so we have the daunting task to encourage, build up, love on, and speak life.

Too bad that these girls never took the opportunity to find out what God thinks about them; they would be so much further along. They are here now, and only God is going to change their outlook. Thank you, Father, that you loved me enough to call me, convict me, and correct me, but mostly you showed me you!

Thank you, Jesus, for helping the girls look amazing! But then you created them. One of the babies ran a fever of 103.2 degree Fahrenheit and then down then back up, so we first of all prayed for her then gave her a bath and medicine then it finally came down, but not without her throwing up on several people in the process.

One little guy saw us stepping over the mess in the floor, so every step he took he lifted his foot to avoid it as well. He didn't stop doing it, and he just kept lifting his foot everywhere, which lightened the mood for everyone.

Thank you, Jesus, she got better. God reminded us that these young babies are so impressionable that they mimic everything they see, so we need to reach out to them in love. I sometimes wonder how we are doing as examples. Father, forgive me if I don't mimic you, the only example they need to follow.

"Let no one despise you for your youth, but set the believers an example in speech, in conduct, in love, in faith, in purity" (Timothy 4:12, ESV).

Trying Toddlers

Did I mention snow...yeah it started again, guess God is really working in the lives of these young ladies. We showed the girls, under our care, how to redirect the kids instead of punishing them. We taught one child, who was two years old, how to use sign language when he couldn't speak very easily. Still another child wasn't eating healthy, only starch and sugary items, so we gave him only vegetables first and the rest of his food after. The mom was worried that he was going to starve. This child hadn't missed many meals so he was okay. After about forty minutes and nothing else was being offered he ate the vegetables. Amazing? I think not. What was amazing was that the mom allowed me to work with him since she knows everything? Next, it was time to work on the moms, and this was no easy task. Thank God he gave me great ideas.

One mom calls her child baby all the time, which in turns makes him whine and act like a baby, so I suggested that she call him by his name and only his name and quit talking to him like a baby, so he will grow up and act properly.

When this child got down from the chair, I asked him to pick up the food that he had thrown on the floor and throw it in the trash. He quickly did what I asked and gave me a high five when he was done. I asked the mom, now wasn't that better, he did what he was asked and felt like big kid doing it? Next, another mom held her baby obsessively and this baby would scream when she finally would put her down. The problem here is that this child should have been crawling two months ago. She didn't want her to be upset for a minute, so she would hold her. She wasn't doing her any favors. So every time we got a chance we put this one on the floor, the mom would try and pick her up. I reminded her of where she would be in a few weeks if given the opportunity to grow. We stretched her and worked her every way she could.

The child responded by the end of the night and was using muscle she hadn't before. Then I had to talk about not picking the baby up during the night because she is not helping either one of them out, as this child was going on eleven months.

She said it would be hard, but she would try, I told her to just think about a good night's sleep for you after two or three days, how would you like that? Next was our newest mom with two kids. She had an attitude and was disrespectful, but we took everything in stride. By just having a baby your emotions would be all over the place, and not to mention, very negative emotions, so we try and give her some direction.

She isn't listening to that, because none of us have been in her shoes. We suggested some ideas for her oldest, and she felt like we were picking on her. So we asked her how we could help, but of course she doesn't need any. About this time the counselor for the girls comes in—ha-ha. Now, she had to use our help because she couldn't have the babies in the room with her. We stepped in and got to work. Maybe, we couldn't ask her, tell her, suggest to her, but now…thank you, Jesus, we could show her!

Her oldest boy started to throw a fit and sat himself on the floor. To time out he went. Her newborn is tired…tired of everyone holding her, so I put her down and she went right to sleep. It's back to time-out king. I tell him until he stops crying, he will just have to sit there. So he stops after about two minutes…yippee. These kids are smarter than you give them credit for. So, next, he tried to hit someone, back he went, and then he throws a toy at a kid. You know the routine. Then he went for the curtain, needless to say, the chair beckoned him again, then to the computer, which were hands off, so to I needed to say it again? Then he pulled the plug protector out of socket, so back he went to the chair, then he threw his apple, and milk, so every time I let him out I explained to him what he did wrong and not to do it again. I can't be mad at the little fellow, because everything is new and nothing being repeated. Now all of this was in a matter of fifteen minutes, but this time the mom came out and she was upset because her son was in time-out, but I asked her to let me finish and she did. So I asked him to come to me after time-out, and he did. I told him what he did wrong, and he went right off to play.

Next, he decided that he was going to take the baby's bottle while mom was trying to feed the baby, so back to time-out, because he threw another fit. All the while mom was watching, I asked if he was ready to get out of time-out, and he looked at me as I told him, "If you want out say, please." So he did. He used his sign language and said please. Then when I was done talking to him he used sign language again, and said thank you. Mom smiled…thank you, Jesus, you finally got through to her.

At the dinner table, he didn't throw his food, he said please, and thank you, and we saw a change in mom. Now, we can't say that tomorrow we wouldn't have to do this all over again, but what else do we have to do, but affect these babies, and mommies lives. I did talk to my sister, and while she is going through a tough time…divorce is always hard. She is going to an incredible church, and God is moving in her life.

Thank you, Father, for loving her through all of the pain, and for comforting and strengthening her walk. It's so hard when we have been away so long, but thank you Father, she is coming back. She always had a beautiful heart, now, and it can be filled with you. Thank you so much for her life, and what it will mean in the kingdom of God. Thank you, Jesus, for this wonderful amazing day, formed by you!

Our Rainbow

Have you ever been in a rainbow? We were driving back from Texas, and we had driven all night and very eager to get home. We had been discussing, who we would like to bless with our ministry. We saw ahead of us about a half-mile away that it was raining pretty hard. As we were approaching the rain, we saw a rainbow.

I immediately said thank you, Jesus, for the all the blessings we are going to have by the end of the year. The rainbow then moved down to the other side of the highway and immediately on us. No kidding the rainbow stayed on us for like five seconds. It literally rested on our car on the left side of the front driver's side. Ron and I were like OMG. Thank you for the sign again. I looked at Ron and said, "Did you see that?

I said did that really happen?" He said, "Yes, why didn't you get a picture?"

I said "we'll I was in the moment, and all I could do was be in awe of what God was showing us."

So I called Michelle and told her. She said really, that's cool.

That wasn't enough so I called our dear friend in Tucson, because she could relate to what had just happened. When we got to her message, another conformation about Gods promises to us, it said. The treasures of heaven will always rest at your door. It was her new recording for her phone, and she changes her messages every day. She couldn't have known that the rainbow had rested on us?

Once again, I was blown away. I was keenly sensitive to God walking around us. But he never does something the same way. He does make it memorable. Thank you…Jesus!

"Now when these signs meet you, do what your hand finds to do, for God is with you" (1 Samuel 10:7, ESV).

Receive, Respond, Repent

What a wonderful day, I got to help with one of the babies who were having a hard time staying asleep. What I mean was this little one decided in the middle of the night that she would wake up and scream at the top of her lungs. Then she wouldn't stop until mom would pick her up, and put her in bed with her. This was not good. Neither one of them would get a good night's sleep.

This was a huge blessing because she came and got me at midnight. You're probably thinking midnight and blessing in the same sentence. It's important to know that this particular girl didn't ask for help. This time she did. I took the baby and put her down in another room. I told her to go to sleep, and she did much to my amazement. Thank you, Jesus. The next day she (baby) was so pleasant, and so happy. See what a little rest could do?

Next was my new mother with attitude. She didn't want anyone around. It's like we were getting on her nerves, and not the other way around. God gave us a wonderful idea to take everyone else to the movies. Snow had stopped, and we could finally get out of the house. She had a very flippant attitude, so Ron took the other girls out while I stayed behind. I reminded her that she had been very rude and disrespectful to everyone in the house. That everyone has been helping her even though she hasn't been nice to them. She started to cry—genuine? I think not. Its so people would leave her alone, so she didn't have to face what she had done. The baby's cried less than she did together. I still tell her what she needed to hear.

Then, I went to work with the other babies that had been left behind, so the moms could enjoy their time away. She came and asked me for favors. I just responded with no, sorry, I don't think so, maybe later…anything to make her have to sit and think about her actions.

After she napped, she decided to help me with the other babies. It was her way of saying I'm ready to work. Now, I would normally expect an apology, but it's tiny steps with these girls, because that's how God is with us—tiny steps until we get it.

You see we are sometimes so quick to want instant change we forget that there is work to be done within. God continually reminds me of his Grace and Mercy, to which we all need to show more of. If I want this girl to respond, God shows me that you can only do so much. Then it's up to the person to receive, respond, and repent.

Thank you, Jesus, she received what I told her, responded by helping others, and you will work on the repenting, in your own time. Thank you, Father, for teaching me through this process, that repenting doesn't come easy, but when it does what a change. Never let me be the reason people won't repent, help me get out of the way, to allow your way!

"But the free gift is not like the trespass. For if many died through one man's trespass, much more have the grace of God and the free gift by the grace of that one man Jesus Christ abounded for many" (Romans 5:15, ESV).

Junk to Jesus

While she was praying with a friend, she was having trouble with her husband. It seems as though she was feeling very discouraged and unloved. God told me to tell her that she was worthy to be loved. That she was created and made for a purpose. That just because her husband says unkind things to her, it doesn't make it true, and that she needs to hear what God thinks about her. When we were done, she was tearing up, and we asked if we could pray with her. As we prayed we asked God to stop her husband from saying any more negative things about her, and that he would not say anything if he couldn't say anything nice.

In the next few days, she told me it was really crazy because her husband hadn't said anything mean or unkind to her. It was weird because, she said, he was anxious, and couldn't figure out why he was feeling this way.

Thank you, God, that you honor our prayers and that they are powerful when we give them over to you. Thank you, God—that this man is coming to know you as his personal savior, and he doesn't even know it yet. Thank you God, that you are moving mightily in this family, and they can see the tide shifting but they can't even begin to know how blessed they are going to be. It was amazing to see this friend smiling, because she finally gets to feel that she is loved –not by her husband but by you. It's life changing. She is leaving a legacy for her children, and it's love!

No longer will her children see her beat down. No longer will her children see her discouraged. No longer will her children see her as less. They will see her full of love, peace, and confidence that comes from her Father. Thank you, Father, for filling her up to overflowing, so that she can be a conduit for her children, who see, feel, and experience God's amazing LOVE!

He Touched Me

God blessed me with an opportunity to talk to another friend, about whether or not she had a testimony, and thank you, Jesus, she did. As she was speaking to me about her testimony, it made her daughter question whether or not she knew Jesus. She didn't have a testimony. It never ceases to amaze me that someone is listening to my conversation who truly is seeking God. Anyway, she asked me to speak to her daughter. As we were speaking, God showed me that she was always seeking him out, but he never really made the decision to follow Jesus.

When I told her that she needed to talk to God to about whether or not she needed to accept Jesus, she sat there, looked at me, and said nothing. After a minute, she smiled and said, "I'm happy, I feel warm." I asked her to repeat what she said. She said she talked to God and said, "God if I don't know you I would like to. Then it happened he filled me with this warm feeling and I'm happy."

She then said it's real; this is what it's about. She went over to tell two people what just happened to her. She got to share with one more because she just couldn't keep quiet. Now, see, that's the difference when Jesus comes in—you can't keep silent about what he has done for you. God does make you feel different, but we never go by feelings. She had to have known Jesus before she could share Jesus.

Thank you, Jesus, for another soul saved, for the confidence in knowing that she knows she has you living in her heart. I get so excited seeing people come to a saving knowledge of Jesus. Thank you, God for giving your son Jesus, so we could have a new life.

"Jesus answered him, "Truly, truly, I say to you, unless one is born again he cannot see the kingdom of God" (John 3:3, ESV).

Trust the Master

There is a knock on the door; it's the same girl who just minutes later dismissed me. Her baby is covered in splotches all over her neck, arms, and face. It is really bad, so I make sure she can breathe. Then I tell her to give her a bath because she has gotten into something she is allergic to.

This mom is very emotional and panicked, which is normal for her. She, however, upsets her babies, even more because she doesn't stay in control. She cries, screams…dang more screaming I thought we put those to bed. At this point I tell her to give her a bath to wash off whatever came into contact with her skin. She does and it starts calming down, but just to be sure we take her in at 11:00 p.m. If we had waited only ten more minutes, we would have seen it all clear up. But it was nice to verify that it was only external and that it was the lotion she had put on her earlier.

The doctor tells her not to wash the baby but every three days to help the natural oils build up on her skin. She tells the doctor okay. I quickly said did you hear what he said she said yes give her a bath every day. I quickly asked the doctor to repeat himself; he said no she only needs a bath every three days nothing more.

She said well I like the way she smells when she gets a bath. He said then spray it in a bag, and sniff it because she doesn't need it. The reason I let him explain is that we know nothing. We can't tell them anything, until someone else confirms that what we said is true. So now at midnight, we are headed home, thank you, Jesus, that there was nothing truly wrong with her baby. So why is it that we trust others that don't even know us over the ones that know us because they have authority? So what gives them authority? It is their dedication to fine-tune their skills and to become masters of their craft. Thank you, Father, that you have mastered everything, and that all we have to do is trust you, because you know it all.

"The LORD is the everlasting God, the Creator of the ends of the earth. He does not faint or grow weary; his understanding is unsearchable" (Isaiah 40:28, ESV).

Haircuts I Hate 'Em

Our friends from Nebraska call. They tell us they are coming in this weekend to go to the concert with us. Thank you, Jesus! We put our heads together and came up with a plan, so that all the babies would be watched, and we all could go. Then I had to break down and get a haircut. Now I'm not a big fan of haircuts, because I can never get the same haircut twice. Even though I have the same hair, I never seem to find that one person that can do it right.

This time it's a guy. I have thick hair, the kind that everyone wishes they had. He says he is going to cut an inch off but it's more like six. Thank goodness my hair grows fast, or I would have been livid. I go home real quick and try and fix it, but it is just not right. Ron says go have him cut it some more, what? More, he already cut off six inches, and you want more to come off—no way. I have to go back because I have to pay him. They only take check or cash. As I got back I showed him how uneven it was. He asked me to sit down, apologized for not looking closer, and fixed it. Now I was still not as happy as I could be, but considering it was so much better, which means in two weeks I will love it.

That's just the way we women are. We have to have time to adjust to change; that's why God goes so slowly with me. Then I got a call from our associate who told me that one of our girls was about to explode. Can we come and talk to her? As we talked to her, she must have felt that we were ganging up on her, but it was quite the opposite. She had so many people that care about her and want her to do well. That's why we take the time to correct what she was doing, so she wouldn't get in deeper over her head. She was changing so much and she had done such a fine job, but just like all of us.

If we aren't changing to God's image then we are falling away. Change is never easy but it is required, because God has so much more for us if we are willing to change. So just like my haircut, I changed it today. As I grow with it, I see so many possibilities that I will soon come to accept and even love the change. Thank you, God, that with your help we are able to love the change as we continue to grow.

You're On

I woke up early, mostly, because I never went to sleep. My guess is God is trying to talk to me. I always want to hear from God, no matter what the time. It's really awesome that I would rather hear from God than sleep. I'd rather wait on God than make a move in the wrong direction.

So how do we hear from God? I see lives being touched with only God being the answer. Things that should break down don't, and places we go we have an opportunity to minister in a way that draws others to Jesus.

I have a dog-named Buster 2.0. Now, it doesn't matter if I am sitting watching TV, taking notes at the table, or talking to someone on the phone, because he likes to be right where I am, watching my every move. It's like he cannot be comfortable unless he knows I'm okay.

Let's think about God for a minute, how he never sleeps, never grows weary of watching, and never quits on interceding on our behalf. What I mean is that he never, never, never stops trying to show us, teach us, the amazing love he has for us. He is on!

I'm so grateful that when I'm not on, he is. God wants that relationship to be so strong that we know he's on, and we can take comfort in knowing we can relax because he is right there! Thank you, God, for allowing me to know, that you are on!

"I saw the Lord always before me, for he is at my right hand that I may not be shaken" (Acts 2:25, ESV).

Paid in Full

One day I decided I wasn't going to do youth group unless God provided for the gas. Michelle called and told me that I had $35 coming to me from last year for a basketball tournament, too funny, guess I will be going to youth. As I was obedient to his will, the heavens opened to pour out a blessing. I was so overwhelmed that I couldn't sleep for two days. God, I'm so honored that you would allow me to be used to reach countless with your story. Thank you, Father, for using me!

We had no money to take our trip to Hawaii. Though we had the tickets, they were from Dallas, and we lived in Atlanta, Georgia. Then two days before we needed to go, God blessed us with some money to take on our trip. Please, forgive me, Lord, for doubting for one minute that you weren't going to do everything on time.

We had a Wal-Mart card, so we used it coming and going, and we never needed the money for gas. We only had a $200-limit, but there is in no limit to God's blessings. We made it to Hawaii without missing a beat. Hawaii was beautiful, and so were the people we were visiting. I was asked to go get the girls from the hotel and was trying not to use the GPS, mostly, because I didn't have it with me and I didn't want to go back and get it.

We all like to go out on our own sometimes and throw caution to the wind. Now isn't that funny how we all used to use maps to get around, and now we had to have a little small voice guiding us? Too funny, we all have that little small voice inside of us; we just need to pay attention. I got to a point where I was asking God if I was supposed to turn left, and as I looked up there was a NO left hand turn signal, to which I said thank you, God, for helping me get there. I went forward two more streets, and sure enough I found my way.

Isn't it neat when we listen to God—how he guides us through our journey and we don't need to be anxious or worry whether or not we will get where we are going, because God will direct our path? Thank you, God, for your wonderful reminders. Then as girls do on vacation I went to look for T-shirts for friends. I parked in a parking lot that I wasn't supposed to park in unless I was a customer. We went to the store and they had nothing, but God reminded me that Michelle needed some juice for her health, so we went into the store and got juice, and just as we were coming out the security was checking our car to have it towed.

Thank you, Jesus, that we were customers of the store, and we didn't even know we were going to need anything when we parked. God always has a way of working things out even if we don't. We did the right thing, in the end because God made sure of it. Thank you, Lord, for this wonderful trip for allowing us to have every cent when we got back, because we needed it for other things. We didn't pay for food, hotel, and travel while we were there. We didn't pay anything; God paid it all. But isn't that just like him to pay it all?

Choose Love

We accomplished a lot with all the errands. We even got some extras especially for one of the girls who just got her hair cut. She transformed overnight and what a change. It's funny how one small thing can make a difference but it does.

I got woke up at 3:20 a.m. by the newest member of our cottage telling me that her water broke. Her labor pains were five minutes apart. By the time we got to the hospital, they were two minutes and she was dilated to seven, so we were just in time.

She gave birth to a boy 8.6 oz. 21 inches long. Why anyone cares about the size and height is beyond me. We know God is going to grow them into the adults they are supposed to be. We just get to watch the process and hopefully make a difference where we can. Thank you, Jesus, for a healthy baby and a mother full of you!

I went to the hospital to get our newest mommy and baby. It took four hours to get her checked out. The problem is that her mom was there telling her daughter that she was doing a terrible job. That she would end up losing the baby. What in the world was she thinking? These new moms need to be encouraged every step of the way, and not brought down, so they feel less than what they are.

I asked the mom, "Can you tell me something good about your daughter?"

She said "No."

I reminded her of how good she was doing and how sweet her daughter was. She replied it's because she wants something. Too bad she will miss out on seeing her daughter become this amazing mother to her child. As we were leaving, I reminded her that it wasn't what everyone else thinks about you; it's what God thinks about you. You are special, precious, amazing to God, and he loves you. So think on those things because they are what really matter.

Thank you, Father, that you see more, and love more! It was a hard day for one girl, difficult day for another, and restful still for the last one. How in the world can we get all of this out of one day? All these girls are in different places in the walk. They are growing as parents, growing as adults, and growing in the grace and knowledge of Christ. The neat thing is they all get something every day if they choose to receive it. Lord, help them all to receive fully the love that you have for them no matter the day they are having.

Direct Our Steps

I was feeding a baby as the other mothers were all outside on the back porch with their children. I would normally feed in the dining room in case there was a mess. I decided I would go into my apartment that is connected to the cottage to get comfortable. I was just about to sit down in my apartment when another one of the toddlers came walking by my door, heading for the streets. Normally I wouldn't have been in my apartment, but the baby needed a quiet place. God needed me to be able to look outside at just that moment. This toddler is not supposed to be anywhere but the back porch and he is in the front by the street. I grab him up.

Thank you, Jesus, that you direct our steps! I sat him down on my chair and waited for mom to discover that he was gone. It took fifteen minutes. When she did she was beside herself.

Thank you, Father, that you protect us all even when we don't know we need it. I was up at 5:00 a.m. Yes, people wake up that early. I wish I hadn't been one of them, but then it was quiet time for me. To reflect and see all that God was doing.

I had to go to the hospital because one of the babies is getting tubes. It's not a big deal, but then it is for the mom. She doesn't know how God works; she is a new Christian and hasn't completely figured out everything God does. I'm older and neither have I. So I reassure her that she will be fine and talked her through it. It's neat to see how her confidence comes from what I say. My confidence comes from knowing when God speaks; I can take comfort in knowing that his word is true. That at every moment in my life God has gently reminded me, He is there and that everything will be just fine...what a difference coming from the Father!

"In the fear of the LORD one has strong confidence, and his children will have a refuge" (Proverbs 14:26, ESV).

Filled to Overflowing

God worked out everything from my credit to the payment for us to get a new RV. Thank you, Jesus, for interceding for us and finding favor with a business that could care less about us. They fixed it, and we were off and running. We left for Dallas and picked up our new RV. We got everything we needed, and we were fixing to drive off when we remembered. Okay, GOD reminded us that we needed a tag so we would be legal. So we turned around, got the tags, and headed from home.

Thank you, Jesus, for helping us to get the RV, which is just another step in your plan. We got to a small town just about thirty minutes from our town. They had an RV park there so we stopped and set up. Now I know we always have to tweak every RV we have ever had, so that was to be expected. One was a pipe in the kitchen sink—it leaked. The mattress was awful harder than rocks. Now I'm supposed to be grateful for everything God supplies, but I was not grateful for this one. Then the couch had a bar that ran down the middle of it, which if you sat on it would hurt. I managed to sit on that bar several times; it seemed to be the only place I sat. Ouch! Then Ron took a shower and water drained out of the bathroom into the bedroom where the heater that was on the floor was. Thank you, Jesus, that it didn't catch on fire…whew!

It needed some calking that was an easy fix. Now if you think about it, that isn't much. By the evening, I was saying to God I hated the RV. All the while Ron was saying what a blessing it was. It was crazy how two people can see something that's totally different?

Father, forgive me. I know this RV blessed us and anytime I complain; I feel like the Israelites that complained even though they knew you were guiding them and watching over them. I know you will take care of even the small stuff, because you pay attention to detail. Father, please help me to be more grateful. I never want to complain over what you are blessing.

God also lined us up a place to store the RV. It worked out perfect, because there were lots of storms going through Oklahoma—hail and tornados, but they never hit that area.

To think this time last week I didn't have an RV. I forgot what blessing it was, this beautiful RV—new, loaded, and now a place free to park it. All the things we thought was wrong were an easy fix. The men on campus offered to help fix things for us. You see how good God is? We are surrounded by gifted men that can help us with anything we need. It was really neat to see a glimpse of how connected we are to each other. The whole time off, God put us in the right place, at the right time to receive everything he had for us. We are so full of your favor it's overflowing.

"When you give it to them, they gather it up; when you open your hand, they are filled with good things." (Psalms 104:28, ESV)

You Forgot to Smile

We did so many errands especially for one girl, and somehow we managed to get it all done. Thank you, Jesus, that every time we needed to be some place we were. Then as I was going to one place I saw a roll of stoplights, you know the kind. You seem too have hit every red light on every block. There were at least thirty, so we might as well have fun.

I was doing a fifty-yard dash with this one car trying to see who could get to the next red light the fastest. This went on for about seven lights. As he got to the next light he moved over to turn left, lucky guy he was done with the lights. He turned on his inside lights and rolled down his window…to my surprise it was a police officer. He told me to slow down because the speed limit was 25…oops!

Then he drove off, thank you, Jesus, that I didn't get a ticket, the officer was probably enjoying the moment as well. I know we didn't show a good example to the girl in the car, but she was laughing the whole time. Sometimes, I think people miss all the fun in life, by not just enjoying it. Thank you, Father that I get to be around kids that bring so much joy it overwhelms me. Thank you for letting them see us mess up, but it doesn't defeat us.

"For it is God who works in you, both to will and to work for his good pleasure" (Philippians 2:13, ESV).

Exciting Easter

We received many calls celebrating Easter. However, I didn't go to church. I stayed up too late and was feeling bad. I hate missing church because I miss hearing the word of God. Michelle called and told me that she invited one of her friends and he came. This is huge, because when he was young, someone in the church told him to get out. He laughed at someone getting baptized, because the kid jumped in the water instead of walking down in the water. Her friend was seeing such a change in my daughter he was willing to give it a try.

Thank you, Jesus, for opening his heart, so he can hear the gospel, and plant seeds in his world as well. Then Ron came out and gave devotion. It was the best Easter story I have ever heard. Here's what he shared: "When we accept Jesus, we have been given life. Sin still reigns in the world, so every day we need to choose life. Will Christ be Lord of your life today?"

Wow! I never got it till this Easter. Thank you, Jesus, for opening my eyes even in my own living room. It was the best Easter I celebrated with everyone I came into contact with. We have the greatest gift of all Jesus!

"Jesus said to her, "I am the resurrection and the life. Whoever believes in me, though he die, yet shall he live" (John 11:25, ESV).

Pray for Steven

As I got up one morning and was going for my walk, when the Lord told me to pray for Steven, this was someone I knew who was always so difficult to deal with, and I had to work with him all the time. We all have a person that makes us grind our teeth. Every morning, I would go to the track, walk two miles and spend my time praying and talking to the Lord. As I was walking, God told me to pray for Steven. I was like whatever. Okay. Watch over Steven. Amen.

The next day came and the Lord told me to pray for Steven. I said, "Okay. Watch over Steven today. Amen."

That was all he was going to get because he didn't even deserve that. On the next day, the same thing, and the next, and the next, and the next! Now this went on for several weeks. Every day like clockwork pray for Steven. After six weeks, I was beginning to get it. I began to pray a little more.

"Watch over Steven and help him to have a good day."

Thinking that I had done him well I figured I was done. On the next morning I heard God say, "Pray for Steven." Well, dang, what does he want? So I would pray and go through the motions. I figured one of us would give up. This went on for four months, and my prayers were still not enough; but then I would add more to my prayers figuring God would quit and give up.

As time went on, I was praying more for Steven and starting to add words that were genuine. Now, it's been seven months, and I woke up and God not wanting to waste time says, Pray for Steven. Only this time, it was different, the words seem more urgent. As I began to pray, I started to weep.

I said, "Father I ask you to draw Steven to yourself. That you meet his needs mentally, physically, spiritually, and financially, and when you do, let him see you in all your glory! Bless his coming in and going out. Put a hedge of protection around him and keep him from harm. Allow him to be the kind of Godly man that will draw his family and friends to you. Touch him for today and for the work that you would have him do. Let it bring honor and glory to you now and forever. Let Steven fall in love with you every day of his life and serve you with his whole heart. We ask this all in Jesus name Amen!"

I even prayed for his whole family: aunts, uncles, mom and sister—everyone that had ever wronged the kids and me. The next day I woke up and God didn't tell me to pray for him even though I did. During the next two weeks, Steven ended up in the hospital. Michael called me. He was all upset and asked if I could pray with him—for Steven.

I said sure and I prayed with Michael. Now just think if God hadn't allowed me to heal through this time, I wouldn't have been able to pray with my son. We wouldn't have gotten to see Steven healed. Mostly that I want to be the loving, caring, compassionate person God designed me to be. Thank you, God, once again for seeing the bigger picture and helping me to show genuine concern for someone else.

God wasn't worried about Steven; he was changing my heart. With every prayer God was concerned with the condition of my heart and making me realize it is a privilege to pray for others, and the greatest thing you can do for them. What's more important is it changes you! Thank you, Lord, for changing me through the process and making me realize you love him just as much as me, whether or not I love them at all. Help me to love those that are unlovable, which includes me.

"Pray without ceasing" (1 Thessalonians 5:17, esv).

Enjoy the Ride

One of the privileges we have with working with teenagers is to get them ready for adulthood. I started with Tina just learning how to do her laundry properly. Then she progresses to learning some cooking skills. Then she goes shopping for groceries, and then working a job to save money. Now all of this is pretty boring, but as I talked to Tina I reminded her that when she would do all these things she could learn to drive. OUCH!

I tell Tina we are going to start off in a parking lot mostly working on braking. This is an art, because when she first started driving she hits the brakes I now have whiplash. I tell her gently imagine there is an egg on the dashboard, and you're not trying to crack it. Then after about forty times stopping, she asks if I can give it the gas now, NO! Not yet we are done. She looks at me and says is that it the gas pedal? Yes, yes it is because in my mind if she can't brake properly she won't be cautious when she is driving with cars. Remember "CRASH" well she's not going out like that. She will know what a brake and a gas pedal are, and why we use them. I might be overcautious, but then this girl isn't. Next, we drive around a circle, she can't hurt anyone, and she can get some confidence. Really, it's me needing the confidence. Did I say she couldn't hurt anyone, let me say she didn't hurt anyone physically?

But she did damage me emotionally. I am wreck and she was only doing ten miles an hour. As she's driving she runs into a curb, then into a drain, and over a toy. Now she hasn't gone one time around the circle. I see kids walking and I tell her to pull over for fear of their lives. She wondered why we pulled over because she asked. I told her need to go over some things before we keep going. Hasn't she already gone over enough stuff? I asked her where she was looking. She said I was looking at my speed. To which I think *what about the road?* I remind her she has to keep her eyes on the road, so she doesn't hit anything. She said that makes sense.

Now this girl is not ready, just like me. I recognize it, because I saw that in myself. I tell her we will keep practicing in the circle and when she is ready we will go out to the streets. She is happy with her results, I'm happy this lesson is over. Now you have to ask yourself this question. How in the world would anyone think they did well, with the driver gasping, stomping her foot on the passenger side even though there is no brake. Then grabbing the door, dash, and handle above the door, not to mention me closing my eyes. But, like everyone else they see one thing, we see another. We then got to take her for a driving lesson, which she was smiling from ear to ear...I, on the other hand, was freaking out, she needs lots of practice...LOTS. She will get there, and I feel like she will be a very competent driver. I'm just happy I'm not in the car with her right now. Thank you, Father, for showing me I think I'm doing okay, when in reality I need lots of work. God you show me that you are patient to get me where I need to be, and allow me to take the wheel as you gently watch over me.

Keys to the Kingdom

I lost my keys again. I'm sure you have heard this before, because I have done this before. I had to get the keys from Rob to be able to drive one of our girls to work. When I got back, Rob and Cindy asked if we could come over and help take down some border across the top of the ceiling. The border must have come over with the ark. No kidding it was stuck and wasn't giving up anything without a fight. Now you have been in those homes where the border is barely hanging on and you could just blow and it would come off. Not here and not now. They must have used cement, glue, and even super glue! They needed to use this stuff for dentures.

But Cindy did some research and came up with a great way to get the catlike claws border down. So between me, Rob, and two other youth we got it all down. Thank you, Jesus. Can I tell you how fast I bolted out of there so I wouldn't have to clean up the HUGE mess we made? I was like lightning—flash I was gone!

Then I left to get our girl from work, when I got back I was asked to come to a back room where another new girl was sitting. Cindy asked me if I would talk to her, so I did. It was easy she was lonely, and I know she needed a friend. So I introduced her to her new best friend, JESUS. After talking a little bit, she decided she wanted to pray, and accept Jesus into her life. I was not expecting this one, but I was sure glad God granted me a front row seat. I wouldn't have missed it for anything. It started out with me focused on keys, and ended up with me focused on the key to the kingdom. I really can't top that. Another one added to the kingdom. What an amazing God we serve...I am in awe!

"I will give you the keys of the kingdom of heaven, and whatever you bind on earth shall be bound in heaven, and whatever you loose on earth shall be loosed in heaven" (Matthew 16:19, ESV).

Glad You're Here

Enter a new girl named Deb, and I did not really want her to be in our house, because I thought she was trouble. Now, get this, all of these kids come with trouble, so why is this one any different. I'm not sure. Everything she brought was full of smoke. We did laundry for twenty-four hours, just something else for me not to like this child. Then God opened my heart and eyes to truly see this child, and she was amazing.

She was very helpful, very kind, and humble, which was something I hadn't been to her when she got there. Then the words came out of my mouth that I had never heard coming out of my mouth, with any of the girls, "I am so glad you are here, you are so special. I'm glad to have you here."

Wow, amazing what will come out of your mouth when you allow God, to speak through you. It made me smile! Father forgive me for looking with my own sinful nature, and not showing her the tenderness, mercy, and grace that you continually show me; thank you for this wonderful amazing, loving, tender, humble, thankful, beautiful child, made by your loving hands. Isn't that the way we should see every one?

We took the youth to the dentist, another youth to the DHS. Then to wind everything up, we took Deb shopping. If anyone needed some clothes it was her. It was the easiest inventory I had done, everything was zero, zero pants, zero shoes, zero under garments, zero coats, she did have shirts but most of them were questionable. We first went to Wal-Mart to get her a haircut. I asked her if she would like to get the hair out of her face she said, "No not really."

I asked her why? She said, "I am ugly, my mom told me all the time that I was ugly."

I told her that's a lie. Let me tell you what God thinks about you. You are beautiful, and he made you perfect just the way you are.

She just looked at me and said, "Well I trust you, so if you think I need a haircut I will get one." While she was getting a haircut, I got underwear, socks, under garments and bottles for her baby because he only had two. When I came around the corner she walked out, and I said, "Wow, you look incredible."

She smiled for the first time. We then went to Old Navy where she got shirts, shorts, pants, jeans, and a much-needed jacket. She had never been into any store but Wal-Mart, so she was a little overwhelmed. Next we went to Target, where they had the Converse shoes that she always wanted. We got her two pairs, and as we were checking out, she had a tear in her eye.

When we got to the car she said, "I have never had this much stuff my whole life, and you guys are amazing."

I said, "No, God is amazing. He brought you to our campus because you needed someone to show you how special you are, and how much God wants to bless you."

She started crying and said, "Is there anything I can do for you?"

I have worked with children for over thirty-five years, and not once has any kid asked me if there was anything they could do for me…I was speechless! For those of you that know me, you know, this is a miracle. So, this is what being grateful looks like. Thank you, God, for allowing me this time, and opportunity to show her Jesus! Then I got an opportunity to talk to Deb about Jesus. Ron had talked to her on Monday when she got here.

That evening she went to church and as the youth pastor was talking, she turned to the girl beside her and said, "I just have to get JESUS." She prayed and accepted Jesus into her heart. Wow, imagine I was ready to write her off. God just keeps blowing me away. I am so grateful that God let me see her through your eyes.

Thank you, Jesus, for becoming real to her physically and spiritually. I just love you so much! Just think about another one of your children pouring out love for you, and is the best life Deb could ever hope for. Thank you for allowing me the opportunity to be a part, and love just another one of your amazing creations!

"But seek first the kingdom of God and his righteousness, and all these things will be added to you" (Matthew 6:33, ESV).

Just to be Close

Time in Oklahoma was up for us. We knew God was leading us somewhere else. We went to this one campus in Georgia to apply. We dearly loved everything about it. The director wasn't at the place to hire people just yet, and we weren't going to be there for a few weeks since we were going to Hawaii. So it worked out perfect for us. Then Michael and Ashley decide that they are done with the campus they are working for, so they accept a position in Florida.

Yippee that just means they are going to be closer to us. When they get to Florida they found out this place wasn't what they claimed. So they turned the position down. It was at this time that the Georgia director calls us up, and is ready to hire us. We are working on some other things, and have to tell her we can't. That's when we tell her about Michael and Ashley. We tell her they are wonderful houseparent's, and I know you would love having them on your campus. She said okay, let me call them, and she did.

She hired them right on the spot. It took a couple of weeks for everything to work through but in the process the kids got to hang out with us. Then we got to talk to Ashley about her salvation experience. She talked to us, which was so exciting because she is typically very quiet. As she talked to me, she wanted to know she truly had Jesus as her savior. Ashley bowed her head and prayed and invited Jesus into her heart. Then we got to share with them how God was going to use them, and how to share the gospel. They were both open to everything that was being said.

As we visited with the kids, they all expressed that they would like to get baptized. Next weekend we are going to the river and having a good old-fashioned baptism service, praise God. This is a new chapter for them, and they even found a church they will be going too. Thank you, God, for opening so many doors and putting them in the place to receive them. Thank you, Lord that they are so close to us once again, and but even closer to you!

"Train up a child in the way he should go; even when he is old he will not depart from it" (Proverbs 22:6, ESV).

Look to God

My daughter came for a visit. I thought it was going to be fun. However, as we got back to the house, Ron and I decided that we would fuss at each other. We have all been there, and it's never the right time to have a discussion in front of everyone, but then that's just what happened.

Ron was tired and hadn't eaten all day and it was already 4:30 p.m., and it wasn't going to get any better until we rectified the situation. Michelle was upset and said I want you to know this is not what I am changing my life for. I have prepared mentally, physically, and emotionally to come here. All I want to do is cry. I only wanted her to calm down but that took a minute. I was feeling a little unsure myself after this little ordeal.

The next morning my friend called and reassured me that everything was going to be fine. God opened my eyes to the fact that I hadn't read my Bible the day before. I hadn't spent anytime truly talking to him. While I was speaking what I know God is doing in our lives. I sure didn't see any evidence, that's when my faith took over. As I listened, things came full circle. Michelle had gone with Sara, and texted me that she was going to move to Georgia.

I thought to myself, *wow...in fifteen minutes God turned everything all around.* Michelle and I were both ready to leave, both ready to take jobs somewhere else, both unsure of what we should be doing. God quietly allowed us the time to hear from him. God gave me back my peace, my joy, and my directions. Silly me, just like Peter when he took his eyes off of God he started to fall. I tell you the truth, it was a horrible feeling, feelings like you're stuck, and you start doubting everything in just that one moment. The moment I turned to God he reassured me, and walked me through it.

Then on Saturday we were all sitting around in the living room and for the first time since Michelle had been there we prayed and everything was right. Now, I say all this to say, if you're not hearing from God, stop and listen. If you're not listening to God get into his word. If you're not comfortable where you are stop and rest. God is working everything out, and while we don't know how things will turn out. We can trust God's timing is always perfect.

Thank you, Father, for continually teaching me I have a lot to learn but you care enough to take the time to teach me, you are so awesome! I love you Lord!

"But as for me, I will look to the LORD; I will wait for the God of my salvation; my God will hear me" (Micah 7:7, ESV).

Clear Picture

Have you ever run the gas tank to close to empty? I was in Hawaii and not familiar of where I was, so before I knew it I was almost out of gas. I had meant to put some gas in the tank before I headed out, but I was in too much of a hurry to stop. Yeah, that's what we do when we think we have to be somewhere that didn't close for three hours.

I was going to only put in $25 but was only seconds from running out of gas. As I got off at an exit, there was nothing around. I prayed to God to help me. I had already stopped and asked different people for directions, and it didn't work. At one point their directions led me through an apartment complex. Unless I was supposed to siphon gas from a car, this wasn't the place. Then as I decide to use my GPS and it re-routes me, and just like that I'm off and going again.

Herein lies the problem, the GPS ran out of power. The GPS wasn't plugged in, and stopped in the middle of the process of re-routing me. Oh NO! My heart is racing, like I had just drunk ten energy drinks. I can't wait for the GPS to start working because I am running on fumes. I go in the direction that the GPS had me go. I hit three red lights and ran two of them. I don't recommend you to do this, but this wasn't my car. I certainly didn't want to have to call anyone to get me gas. The gauge then drops below empty, and I was really stressed now.

I tell God, "look you're going to have to find a gas station soon because I don't know where to go." I have turned the air condition off at this time. I probably should have done that in the first place. It is now dark, and I really don't know the area I am in, and I begin to say, "Please! Please! Please! Help me God."

I turn left, because it's the only way I can go. I drive seven blocks, and to my right in the middle of a neighborhood was a station. Still in a state of panic, I turn in quickly and drive through a parking lot. The parking lot has speed bumps, but I never felt them. I pull in and grab the nozzle and start pumping. As the gas tank begins to fill, my heart calmed down.

Now, I could have avoided all of this mess if I would have just stopped when I was supposed to. Here's something funny, it was just gas, nothing so life threatening, just gas. We tend to make more out of a situation than is really necessary, but, at that time, we are caught up in the moment and can't see it clearly.

Thank you, Lord, that you always have the clear picture and can stay calm. I'm grateful one of us does.

"When the righteous cry for help, the LORD hears and delivers them out of all their troubles" (Psalms 34:17, ESV).

Hawaii Happenings

Once again I wasn't thinking while I was out, trying to get things done, and before I knew it I spent $90. Then I get a call exactly $90 tithed into ministry; the exact amount that I had spent that day for shipping, gas, and eating out, it was totally God. I was asked by Michelle to go back to the flea market in Hawaii to get her dresses. She couldn't decide if she wanted them, and ten minutes before she was to get on the plane she wants them. I was driving around and Seaside Street was brought to my memory. I get to the place where Michelle gets two more dresses. Thank you, God, for always being there and helping to remind me of things just at the right moment.

I was laughing because I was trying to go to the hotel to pick up Margie and Michelle, and I didn't get off of the right exit. When I did turn to where I thought I was supposed to, it was then I ask God to help me find the hotel. It was two blocks later when a detour came up and forced me to turn left. When I did I was right where I was supposed to be.

Thank you, Jesus, for the left turn that got me right to my destination. It is never too late to reach for God. I had spoken to a young man while I was in Hawaii, and he wanted nothing to do with what I was saying. At one point he got upset and walked out of the room. I just let him go and didn't say anything else, because that's where the Holy Spirit came in. We can share our story, and it's up to God to draw them.

As we were getting on the flight back to Georgia, the young man called that I had talked to earlier about Jesus. He decided he wanted to accept Jesus as his personal savior. So, I prayed with him over the phone and he accepted Jesus into his heart. The neat thing was that he apologized about how he acted earlier, and he wanted to take the opportunity to know Jesus. It never ceases to amaze me that God never stops working, even if we are busy doing something else.

Thank you, Father, for one more soul saved and a perfect end to vacation. However we are never on vacation from sharing your story.

Listen and Learn

How many times have you said I wished I had listened to them? My husband is the perfect example of someone you need to listen too. He doesn't do that much talking but when he does, it's worth listening to. One time he had told me to be safe around the kids. Now I'm the fun one so I don't heed his warning. The boys were outside jumping over each other but only instead of leapfrog it was high jump giraffe. The boys would literally jump while the person was standing straight up. It was going well, until that wasn't challenging enough. They decided to go over not three but five guys all standing up. Just like Ron said, someone got hurt. It turns out one of the boys hurt his collarbone. I wished I had listened then. Ron also would tell me that I needed to be in the word more. It wasn't that Ron wasn't willing to teach me, but that there are things that God wants to show you. So once again I didn't listen and hardly read my Bible much.

While I was at church I gave a challenge to everyone that wanted to be a part of reading the Bible through and we would do it together. Since I always want to be a person of my word I began to read five chapters a night.

Wow, the word begins to come alive to me. My prayer life was stronger than ever. Then my steps of faith became even easier. We also got to see more people come to know Jesus. It's all because I got into God's word. Amazing what will happen when you study his word. One time I even got to tell Ron something, and he asked me where it was and I showed him. Big deal for me, even though I had read it before it became nourishment to my soul. I sure wish I had listened then, and I could have been here a lot sooner. I remember him telling me to write a book.

Now I didn't feel adequate enough to write a book since I didn't have the education he did. After talking to several different people, I was encouraged to start writing. I realized that I wanted people to learn and be encouraged by my stories. Maybe, they wouldn't have to go through what I did. Maybe, they need to be encouraged, because they are going through it. Either way I wish I had listened sooner. I might be on my third book by now. Thank you, God, for a wonderful husband that encourages me and teaches me and lets me figure it out.

Ron taught me physically to be safe, to spiritually draw close to God as he emotionally encouraged me. Ron is a husband that cares about my whole being. I'm blessed I have a Father and husband that love me enough to try and help me. Thank you God, for your wonderful words of wisdom and the words you give Ron.

"Draw near to God, and he will draw near to you…" (James 4:8, ESV)

Angels Arrive as God Guides

We prepared to leave one campus to go to another. While it is always hard, it's necessary to stay in God's perfect will. We were in west Texas heading down a stretch of highway that nobody had ever traveled. We had passed several small towns along the way, but they were few and far between. We were no more passed a town, about 20 minutes, when a semi-truck drives up beside us. He was pointing at Ron to move over. We were in the right lane, on a two-lane highway where could we move over too? Well, this guy was persistent. He not only pointed but he started honking as well. We stopped, and so did he.

He got out of his truck and proceeded to walk over to us. As Ron got out of the truck, this guy tells him that we lost a tire about five miles back off of the RV. We were shocked because we never felt anything. The wheel had completely sheared off the lug nuts and there was nothing left. Even if we got the wheel we wouldn't have been able to put it back on. Now reality sets in, the RV should have rolled but God's angels held it up so we didn't get hurt. We call our insurance and they locate a tire shop twenty minutes back. They can't get a tow for our RV because it doesn't cover it. So we call the tire shop and tell them all that has happened. They tell us to bring it over. Really, bring it over; sure we will be right there! They did say they would stay open for us since it was after 4 p.m.

You know everything in small towns closes down after 4 p.m. Well, we decide that if God spared us this far we would be okay to drive it back. We had to drive three miles to find a place to turn around. Then on the way back we were driving so slow that we could have seen ants having babies. When we did find the tire it wasn't any good. They already told us it would be around $400 to fix the pins and anything else that might need to be done. As we were pulling up to this so called tire shop. God began to talk to me.

God said, "We were where we were supposed to be."

I said, "We are in the middle of nowhere."

He said, "Call Andy."

Now, let me tell you who Andy is. Andy was the director from another Children's home we had the privilege to meet just two weeks before. It was in Portales, New Mexico in the middle of nowhere! Did I say nowhere? Well, they had a McDonald's and a Wal-Mart and that was it. He was truly a man of God and doing a wonderful job with the kids. We fell in love with him and thought we would thoroughly enjoy working with his ministry.

I got in the way and told Ron. There is no way God would take us to the middle of nowhere. We kept looking and the place in Arizona gladly welcomed us back. That is why we were headed to Arizona. We forget that Arizona didn't have a place for our RV—forget that we were only relief. Our main reason was that we were only going because they had great things to do there.

So fast forward, I said "but I don't have his number."

The God says, "Yes, you do." Sure enough there was the number still left in my phone. I usually delete numbers after I'm done with them, but not this time. So, it's now 5:15 p.m. Yes, it took us that long to drive twenty minutes back. I call Andy try to get a hold of him. He answers the phone to my surprise. I remind him of who this was, since just three weeks ago we told him we weren't interested in the job.

I tell him, I think we are supposed to work for you. I ask him if he has hired anyone for the job. He said there hasn't been e-mail, phone calls or even an inquiry since we left. I told him where we were, and he said we were thirty minutes away.

Andy said, "You come when you can. The job is yours."

I told him that we probably wouldn't be there until the next day since our RV has broke down. We took the truck and left the RV with the garage, and went and got a bite to eat. We ended up being at a restaurant that served a steak sandwich that Ron loved. The owner just happened to be a Christian. We got to fellowship, and enjoy some wonderful food. Within forty minutes the garage guy calls, and says we are done. I was floored by how quick everything was coming together.

When we got there, he had a new rim, tire, lug nuts, and pins, and he said, "I'm sorry but it is going to cost you $125."

I was so amazed at how God worked everything out. We were thirty minutes away, instead of ten hours. It only cost $125, instead of $400. We were protected even in my disobedience. I was given another opportunity to be in God's perfect will.

Now here's something that we didn't know. When we got to campus there were four RV pads that we could hook up to. Then when we got there, four young men came over to help hook us up. So our RV was in a safe place where we could check on it every day if we wanted to. We worked two weeks and off nine days, who wouldn't like that schedule.

As we found out the blessings just kept coming. Andy asked Ron to preach in different churches around the area since he knew Ron's heart was to be a pastor. Now not only do we get to work with kids, but churches as well. As if we weren't blessed enough, just being in his will, He does this for us. I learned to love the area, because God was there.

Growing Family

As we started working with the church, we enlisted several people to help serve in different areas. In case you didn't know it, churches need everyone working together to function properly. It was at this time that we wanted and needed a music minister. We put the word out in the community, and a young man showed up who was willing, able and certainly qualified. We told him we couldn't pay him, but that didn't matter he was called, and he wanted to serve.

His name was Ron. His mother's name was Brenda, and his dad name was Ron. Ron and Brenda our names, it was funny, but God does have a way of connecting people. He reminded us of our son Michael, he was tall, compassionate, and has a servant's heart. As we got to know him, we found out he was married with a little girl. He wasn't happy in his marriage of five years, and seemed to stay at the church way more than he should. We had several talks about what was going on with his marriage, and like most he was making excuses. He complained that his wife's mother was always at his house, and that she never wants to spend time with him. He told me his wife and him have nothing in common.

As we began to talk we shared with him that he wasn't attending to his wife's life. We told him that if he didn't like the mom always being there, then he needed to be there. He made decisions in his life that he never included his wife. I told him that if I wasn't even considered in a decision for the family then I wouldn't feel very significant. You see women have to feel loved to show respect to a man. Same is true for a man; he wants to be respected before he can show a woman love. It was a catch twenty-two for couples. I told him as a man of God you have to be there for her physically, mentally, and spiritually; if one area is missing then you are going to have to work on it. Something finally clicked, and he started spending time at home with his wife.

Her mother wasn't around as much, because she wasn't needed like before. Ron began to include his wife in their decisions, which made the both of them feel valued. Most importantly, Ron cherished his wife as a friend, companion, and partner. It wasn't six months later that she was pregnant with their second child. Growing in the grace and knowledge requires that you invest your time on attending and watering. As he grew with his family, God grew his ministry.

Thank you, God, for helping us to value the family you blessed us with. Help us grow a generation that wants needs, and desires healthy marriages with loving parents guided by you.

"However, let each one of you love his wife as himself, and let the wife see that she respects her husband" (Ephesians 5:33, ESV).

Fishers of Men

While on campus, we met wonderful couples. All of them had a heart for the children. As we got to know them better, we found out that one of the couples had a car they were trying to sell. We checked it out, since we had a truck that got terrible gas mileage, we wanted to purchase something that we could afford to feed. They only wanted to pay it off, so we looked up the price it was worth twice as much.

We made arrangements and purchased it. We bought new tires, lights, brakes, and a new windshield, which still only added to the value of the car. Now we were ready to go when it came to the car. Michael was a huge blessing, because he fixed everything, which saved us hundreds of dollars. We knew we were supposed to get the car because of all the open doors. We were getting accustomed to the campus and all the kids. Ron and I worked as relief, (we took the regular houseparent's place while they were off) it took longer to get to know the kids in this position.

As we shared with each one of the kids about God's perfect plan for their lives, they opened up. One day, five of the kids in one house prayed and accepted Jesus, and the next day two more. We never realized how hungry the people in New Mexico were for the gospel. We soon found out that 90 percent of the people in New Mexico didn't know Jesus. The People are hungry for anyone to share their faith with them.

By the time we were in the third house, we saw ten kids come to know Jesus as their personal savior. How exciting, we had only been there for ten weeks. It was easy, mostly because we only do what God leads us to do. To think if we had gone to the other campus how many things we would have missed.

Cast Your Cares

As we prepared for friends to visit us, we cleaned up the place. It was nice to have a clean house. Cindy and Rob came in town, just in time for the concert. We left their baby with the neighbors and off we went. When we got there all the seats were full except the nosebleeds' section. Ron couldn't sit that high without it freaking him out, so we went looking for more. We found some behind the stage. It wasn't the best seats, but it wasn't high so it would do.

During the concert I saw Cindy praying, and God told me she was worried about her baby. So when she was done I asked her what was the matter, she told me that she was worried about her son.

God told me to share with her that the enemy was trying to steal her joy. You need to relax and enjoy what God has for you here. She smiled and went back to worshipping.

Thank you, Jesus, for allowing me be at the concert, and see it through someone else's eyes. I've been to so many concerts; I sometimes miss how special they can be.

"Agree with God, and be at peace; thereby good will come to you" (Job 22:21, ESV).

Better Boundaries

We have this group of kids that for whatever reason they hoard food. Some do it because they have done without for so long they consume crazy amounts of food. It is typical, but after a few weeks they slow down and start eating normal. Some have food as their only comfort, so they sneak food. It's not that they are hungry; they just want to make sure they will have some food when they need some. Others take food and hide it, so even if it goes bad they have some kind of control over their lives. Either way this is just one obstacle they have to overcome.

One particular day, we had one kid decide that she was going to take pop tarts. I wouldn't have thought too much about it, but she took eight packages, which was a total of sixteen. We sat all the girls down and asked them who has been sneaking pop tarts? Of course all of them denied it.

We were ready to check their rooms and had a good idea who the culprit was. We sat them down again and asked them which one would like to have their rooms searched first. Everyone but one girl raised their hand to be first. You see the one that didn't raise her hand just looked at the others. Why she didn't raise her hand just to cover her tracks is beyond me. I am thankful that she isn't a good liar. We started searching their rooms. As I got to the one that didn't raise her hand and opened the first drawer, whoa three wrappers fell out. It was like the wrappers were begging to get out. There were more wrappers in other drawers, and more in the bathroom under the sink.

Here's something funny. She had a trashcan, not two feet away, why didn't she just throw them away there? We looked at her and she just smiles sheepishly and said nothing. I'm grateful that she didn't say anything, because when you're caught it's best not to add salt to the wound. Later that day when she got home from school, I decided to take this a little farther and give her a nickname befitting to her. What else but "Pop Tart."

I asked her if she got her fix for today. Cause you're not getting any more of your supply here. She got embarrassed and said, "I'm sick of pop tarts." Only after sixteen you're tired of them?

Then I said, "See the pantry. Well, you can't go in here anymore, because just like addicts they have to keep their distance."

All the while we were laughing. We still call her Pop Tart, and she smiles and shakes her head. You see, sometimes we get what we want even though what we get isn't good for us, or what God wanted us to have.

When we acquired things the wrong way, it gives us no satisfaction. God gives us boundaries, because we can't handle too much at once. We aren't ready for it, and it consumes us. That's why it's a little bit here and there. Otherwise, it will lead to destruction. She ended up gaining ten pounds. The pantry doors have to be locked now, because she lost our trust. She hates and I mean hates pop tarts, but she has to buy with her allowance two more boxes.

It doesn't mean we are disappointed. It just means she made a mistake and hopefully will learn from it. Thank you, God, that while we all don't make good choices, you still choose to encourage us, love us, and guide us to healthy boundaries. Boundaries we need because they help us take things in small amounts, so we can digest them properly.

"When you walk, they will lead you; when you lie down, they will watch over you" (Proverbs 6:22, ESV).

My Pad or Yours

Got up today my tooth was hurting so bad, that I took more medicine two hours early. It ended up hurting worse than if I had let it calm down on its own. Then it was so bad I was crying. I was wondering why I was forced to endure all this pain. I came up with nothing. Ron had gone to the store. We seem to always forget something, so we have to go back. Ron had gone back several times, during this day (I should have gotten frequent flyer miles).

Anyway, Ron forgot his iPad. He had left it on the counter at the store. Now, if you know Ron and me you never see us without our iPad, it's a staple in our lives. It's sad but true. Anyway, he came home, and asked me to help him look for his iPad. It was nowhere to be found, so he knew he must have left it at the Wal-Mart.

Ron jumped in the car and headed down there, so he could possibly hope that someone turned it in. I prayed that he would have it returned, as he was gone. He came back not upset just a little frustrated, because he was silly enough to leave it behind. I was in the bedroom trying to get some relief, when I got a call from a number I didn't know. They asked if I was Brenda.

I said do you have my husband's iPad they said, "Why yes we do."

I said, "thank you, thank you, thank you, my husband uses it to preach from. You can't know what a blessing it is to be getting it back."

Now this had been two hours since he lost it. Ron ran back up to the store met the guy and he told Ron. I was playing with this iPad, and I had this knot in the middle of my stomach and it was hurting. As much as I wanted to keep the iPad, I was scared, nervous, and even anxious to while I had the iPad. It was like I was going to be cursed while I kept it. I knew I needed to try and get it back to you.

As soon as I made the call my stomach quit hurting. It was amazing how God will call things back in your life, and how he will use others to witness to as he does it. The man got a $30 tip, but he was more excited about knowing he did the right thing.

In the end he was blessed with being an example to his kids, wife, and could rest knowing he was an upright man. You can't put a price on that. I prayed God would bless him, because he did right to be a servant of God. God would pour into his life all because of this tiny deed. Who knows, maybe this will draw him to a personal relationship with God. I may never know the young man's outcome, but I do serve a GOOD GOD!

Don't Move

We were woken up with the sound of running water, sure enough our water softener had messed up and water was everywhere. We called a plumber, and he came over to fix it. Now, God sent him, because he wouldn't charge us anything. As he talked he shared with us how he would like to work with youth from every background. He has a summer camp for kids, and he charges nothing for it, sweet!

Later that evening, I got a call from our church saying they couldn't help our kids with any Christmas items. They already funded another ministry. There's no problem, I figured God would open another door, which to my surprise was the plumber that came over early that day. He had connections to several different organizations. He was going to put out the word.

Ron was talking to him and got to share with him a little bit. This guy was mad at God for allowing many of his friends and family over the past year to die—five to be specific. Ron got to visit with him, and we knew God was going to use him to bless us.

The neat thing is that I didn't have to go anywhere. I was sitting in my front room and he walked in. We received clothes, gifts cards, and MP3 players for all the girls for Christmas. That's the kind of God we serve. Don't move I got this!

"Blessed shall you be in the city, and blessed shall you be in the field" (Deuteronomy 28:3, ESV).

I Have a Family

After dropping off one of the girls to school, I came back and read my Bible. As I was reading my Bible, God said look through your work e-mail again. When I did, there was a girl that needed to be placed in a home. I never saw this one before, but it was clear as day, and there it was. I read through her file and was moved almost to tears.

Everyone, including her parents, had thrown her away. It's no wonder she was in the mess she was in. God told me all she needs is to be loved, and she will be the child I created her to be. I called everyone concerned and asked if she had been placed yet, and of course she hadn't. Then I asked if I could go visit with her to see if she might like to come and be a part of our family.

I let Ron read her file, and he said the same thing as I did—she just needs love. When I got to her school I tried to go in one door and a sign pointed around the building. Before it was all said and done, I walked all the way around the building. I said nothing but thought it unusual that I would walk completely around the building before I found the right door to go into.

God reminded me that the people of Jericho had to march around the city once every day. He was preparing them to take the city. I went in the door and asked to speak to April. They took me to her room and called her out of her class. When I saw her I thought she was a boy. I was grateful that I said nothing.

Thank you, God, for allowing me to keep my BIG fat trap shut.

She looked at me and said, "Am I in trouble?"

I said, "Do you usually get into trouble"

She said, "No." I said, "Well, don't worry, now. I would just like to talk to you."

As we sat and talked, she finally asked; "why are you here?"

I said that I work with blessed ministries and I came across your file today. I would like to see if you might like to come and live with our family. She started to get tears in her eyes, and as she did a lady from the front desk came over and sat beside her.

She said to April, "you see God really does answer prayers."

Then April began to weep uncontrollably. Vicki as I later found out was the lady's name. She looked at me as she could hardly talk and said, "Two weeks ago we prayed with April because she asked us to. You see we asked her what she wanted for Christmas. She said all she would like is to be a part of a family. So you see we serve a good God who knew you would come by today and give her the gift that she wanted."

April looked at me and said, "You really want me."

I said choking back the tears, "yes, more than anything else we would love you to be a part of our family. What do you say?"

She said, "Yes, yes, I would love to come and live with you." Still crying she said, "It's really truc. I'm going to have a family." She and Vicki hugged, and I told her that God loves her so much that he made sure that I would come across your file, so that your prayers would be answered. She told me that she received Jesus into her life in October and he has truly changed me. We talked a little more, and I was honored to be in that place at that time, to share in what God was doing. I then took Vicki's information down and met another man working in youth ministers.

My joy was overwhelming me, because of all the connections I was making. I was where God wanted me, even though I was feeling sorry for myself every time I looked at our finances, and wonder why I couldn't work for a place that paid better, and had better benefits. Then God quietly showed me all day, why I am here, to be used by him for his glory! I'm richer than anyone I know. The neatest thing about today was this girl gave me the biggest HUG. It was like she was finally free to express what God was doing in her. The HUG was meant for God, but he allowed me to receive it. I did nothing to earn her gratitude, but thank you God I was rewarded with the greatest gift of all LOVE!

"Those who sow in tears shall reap with shouts of joy!" (Psalms 126:5, ESV)

Paid the Way

We were trading in our old truck that took several gallons of gas to fill it up. With the price of gas going up, it was costing $125 for a tank of gas. I could no longer afford to feed this truck, so it had to go! As we decided to go back to the same car we had before, because it was roomy. Ron wouldn't hit his head, and I could afford to feed it. We got to the dealership and as usual I did all the dealing. Women are good at dealing; they shop for half of their lives. So, why wouldn't they be good at buying cars? We picked it out, signed on the dotted line and were out in three hours.

An interesting thing, we never showed them a check stub, or lied about how much money we were making. We weren't making any money; we were helping start a new church. We had no income but we still walked out with a brand new car. It was God's favor, nothing else. We paid nothing down, and our payments were good. I was hoping for the same payments but $45 more wasn't bad.

A year later we got a notice in the mail saying they messed up on our loan, and we should have gotten a lower payment and lower interest rate. Also because they charged us too high, they sent us a check for $1200 for overpayment. Next they lowered our payment to $45 to what we wanted to pay in the first place. I probably should have gone for even less of a payment. We were out of a job since we were helping start a church. We made no money. God doesn't need money though—he paid our payments for seven months. If you are obedient to God's will. He will move heaven and earth to take care of you. Thank you, Father, for making a way, a way to be paved by you.

"Blessed are the people to whom such blessings fall! Blessed are the people whose God is the LORD!" (Psalms 144:15, ESV)

Kids Know You Care

With all the girls off to school, we were blessed to have a young man that was gifted, and talented to take care of our needs. He has been fixing everything that was broken in the cottage—from doors, to drawers, to trim work, to toilets, and even replaced all of our closet doors in the entire girl's rooms. It was such a blessing to have him here and such a nice young man.

Every day when he got there, there seems to be something else that broke the day before, like one of the toilets, and even our front glass door broke just minutes before he got there...God thing for sure. We love Ron but we know his limitations. He got there at 9 a.m. and left at 6 p.m. He put in a full day, and he smiled all the way.

What a great way to serve others with a happy heart. Then all the babies got home and the screaming began, with two being potty trained. The other just being trained to not being held, everyone was whining... now remind you, not crying...whining. Not a tear fell, just the loud crazy yelling, and it didn't stop until 8:00 p.m., so this went on for five hours. I wish I was kidding, but I'm not. We did errands in between all of this. Needless to say, we had a lot of frustrated moms.

Hey, I'm a mom too! I thought it was the perfect time to write. Yes, I said, write a letter to one of my former kids from where I used to work. I now have a pen pal and this is defiantly a lost art. So, I got a letter off and even managed to send him a picture or two. Kids won't care how much you know, until they know how much you care. Taking a little time to send him a letter helps him through where he is. As I was finishing up the letter, one of the girls walked up and asked for an envelope to mail her letter. She already had an attitude from earlier because she didn't want to clean up the kitchen. I told her she would have to wait, so she says never mind and walks away.

This doesn't bother me, because if you're going to work with kids these days you need to know you're going to get—whatever, never mind, forget it, why me, fine, I know, it's not fair, rolling eyes, and my favorite, the silent treatment. I like this one, but I never get it enough. I go into the apartment and begin to unwind, so I can have my devotion time. I get a call from my friend who tells me that she can no longer have Bible studies with her boys in her house. She is another houseparent from where we used to work.

Anyway, they not only can't have Bible study with the boys but they can't have Bible study with each other either. She is hot, so I remind her that we got written up all the time for sharing the gospel there, so she is in good company. Then I reminded her that she should count it all JOY when she suffers for the sake of the cross, because she is storing up her treasures in heaven. It's really surprising these days when you realize that we live in the third largest evangelized nation. Yeah, they are sending people to us, so that we might hear the gospel, what a shame!

With My Looks

Ron was headed out. Taking one of the younger boys with him, he decided that he would like to stop and get a donut. They had just dropped off all the kids to school and the donut shop called to them as they drove by. Ron looks at the little boy and says would you like a donut. Has there ever been a kid in history ever to turn down a donut? Silly question! They get out and Ron checks his wallet he has no money. He asks Sam since we have no money, I think we can get some donuts on your good looks?

He boldly says, "I can get donuts on my good looks." As they step up to the counter Sam says, "I don't have any money, but can I get a donut on my looks?"

The lady looks down and says sure honey what would you like. He smiled so BIG, and took his donut and sat down to munch.

Ron quietly offered to pay the lady later, but she refused to take any. Ron told Sam I wish I was a good-looking as you so I could get a donut.

He said, "You're not" and kept eating.

Thank you, Father, for always sharing these young lives with us, they are fun and full of donuts.

"Ask, and you will receive, that your joy may be full" (John 16:24, ESV)."

Beautiful Babies

This was the morning I was determined to get up and set our problem child in her place, but God had other plans. She apologized in a letter; it's all some of these girls can do, so I hugged her, and I said all is forgiven.

We got our new table and chairs and they look just beautiful. Thank you, Jesus, it was better than I could have imagined. Then our carpenter came and started on our doors, which he did great! The girls had to go to an independent living class. The babies were left with Ron and me. I think I must have needed to get a taste of motherhood. One boy was doing this and another doing that, while another one was crying and another one was hungry. STOP! That's why they have these babies young. If you weren't young you couldn't do this crazy stuff.

Well, time-out was in order for the little monster boys. Then the little shrieking girls needed to be held. All the while people where coming and going so it looked like the children were in charge instead of us. At one point, Ron said you're getting upset. You need to calm down…I agreed and took five. I know God was trying to teach me that these girls are stressed out at times. With all the demands, it feels like they are caught between a rock and a hard place. I only did this for two hours; they do this day in and day out; so compassion is greatly needed when dealing with these children and their moms.

The girls are young and doing an exceptional job, and they need to hear that more and more. Father, forgive me, for not treating them like you would have. Help me to shower them with love and praises so they see Jesus. We only have to plant seeds that will bring up a harvest in their children. Let it be enveloped in love. Thank you for teaching me every day. I have a lot to learn. Please, continue to do a good work in me.

Designed by Kids

One of the most fun things for me is to share Bible stories with the little kids, trying to make it come alive. One example is Bartimaeus; he was born blind. When I asked Sam what being blind was like, he said he didn't know. I asked him to close his eyes, but being a three-year-old, he couldn't help but open them. He wasn't going to get the full effect, so I blindfolded him. Then I told him to walk from the bedroom into the kitchen. He ran into the doorpost before making it into the hallway. He walked straight down the hallway SMACK into another wall. I couldn't help but laugh, but he wasn't going to stop until he got to the kitchen. I couldn't afford him running into anything else, so I stopped him.

He then said, "This is hard I can't do it. I need help. I don't like being blind."

I pulled off the blindfold and said, "see just like Jesus he healed him so he could see." Sam said, "Jesus is awesome like that. I'm glad the man asked for help or he would be stuck where he was."

We also got to share a story about Zechariah. Zechariah didn't' believe what the Lord had told him about having a son, so he was unable to speak. Kids have no concept of time, so you have to put it in a way that they understood. I explained to him that from the time he started going to school until the time he was out for the summer he couldn't say a word. Then I broke it down further.

Imagine not talking for a whole week? From the time you go to school till you go to church. He was starting to get it. Then I said what if you couldn't talk from the time you woke up to the time you went to sleep?

Then just like God does break it down further. I said how about this— don't say anything at dinnertime; see how hard that would be.

Sam said, "I wouldn't like it. I couldn't tell God thank you for dinner. I would be sad, because no one would know how much I loved them."

Zechariah should have believed God because he told him.

"I'm glad I can talk, because I believe God."

We were sitting down for dinner, and I asked the boys if there was anyone that would like to pray. Everyone was willing so I picked a boy. He started with God is great. God is good. Let us thank him for our food. By his hands we are fed. I stopped him before he was finished.

"Look fellows you are talking to God almighty; the creator of the universe. When you pray you have his undivided attention; and all you're going to do is repeat the same verse you have heard all your life? How would you like it if every time we talked we only said one thing to you? Think about what you are saying, God cherishes every word."

Then I asked, "Is there anyone that would like to pray now."

Sam spoke up and said, "I will do it."

First thing he said was, "Thank you for God."

I can't remember anything else that was enough to leave me speechless. Out of the mouths of babes we see pure love, the kind we desire for our lives. Thank you, God, for allowing me to be a part of their incredible, insightful lives.

Being social is a skill that most of these kids don't possess when they arrive on campus. We work on setting healthy boundaries and what appropriate conversation looks like. Some will be very outgoing and some you can't get to say a word during devotions. We have one girl that we are forever trying to get a simple sentence out of. We encourage her every chance we get. She would prefer to keep her head in a book. No need for makeup, fixing her hair, or brushing her teeth. Just kidding about her teeth! All we ever see is a book with legs.

One particular day, we were all hanging out in the living room. Everyone was listening to music, talking and playing games. In walks our un-social butterfly. She didn't have a book so I'm surprised. She had a deck of cards, so Ron asked her what she was doing.

She said, "I am here to be social."

Ron says wonderful, what are you doing with the cards? Without missing a beat she says, "I'm going to play solitaire."

It was all we could do not to laugh. She is serious. She has no idea what she just said. She is making baby steps every time she steps out of her comfort zone she grows. Thank you, God, that when we step out of our comfort zone, we are never out of yours.

Teach Me

As kids sometime do, they get into trouble. I know you're thinking there is no way those sweet little angels would get into trouble? Yes. When they do, we have to give them consequences for their actions. It's not our favorite thing to do, but it's necessary to teach them valuable lessons. We work harder when they are in trouble than they do. One day one of the youth has to mow and pick up pinecones. We have lots of trees, so the pinecones are plentiful. We tell Robert that he needs to pick up the pinecones in this area and go back to the cottage. An hour later, he comes into the house. We ask him if he is done. He says yes. Then we say, "Well, let's go see what kind of job you did."

He starts telling me as we are walking to the spot. These trees drop a lot of pinecones. We said yes they do. As we walk up on the area he says, wow, look how many pine cones those trees dropped after I left. Now it's all I can do not to laugh. He is trying everything to get out of picking them up. He still had to pick them up. If he had picked them up the first time, instead of just hanging out for an hour, he would have been done.

Thank you, Father, that when we try to get out of things that will help us; you bring us right back to that teaching moment so we get it right.

"I will instruct you and teach you in the way you should go; I will counsel you with my eye upon you" (Psalms 32:8, ESV).

You Need Jesus

While at church, we decided that a group of the youth and us would pass out flyers. We wanted to promote the youth night; we were having at the church. We had kids from twelve to seventeen with a nine-year-old. The nine-year-old begged to come, so we let her. Our plan was to hit four different neighborhoods close to the church. We headed out at 6:00 p.m. It was still light out, so the kids would be seen. I told them I would walk with them. They insisted that they were faster if I just followed in the car. Hey, no problem here—I drive they run, I got this. Several people weren't home, but we left invitations on their doors. It was around 7:00 p.m., I asked the kids if they were ready to quit. They kids said, "no way, we still have flyers!" It was fun for me. I just had to drive and hear the reports. One kid said they slammed the door in her face, so she left the flyer on the door. Another one said they wouldn't even answer the door, and I knew they were in there, but they wouldn't come to the door.

Then another came back and said sure, we would love to come, what time? But the best one came from the little nine-year-old. She came back to the car and said, "Mrs. Brenda they answered the door. I began to tell them about your Friday night youth group, and she said don't bother me. I don't go to church!

"I couldn't help myself; I just said forget church, you need Jesus! She looked at me, and said nothing. Then I handed her my Bible and left."

Now, I have no idea what that did for her, or to her. But I know this, that little girl share with her, what she really needed. She shared Jesus and his word. Thank you, Jesus, that we have everything we need in YOU!

"Go therefore and make disciples of all nations, baptizing them in the name of the Father and of the Son and of the Holy Spirit" (Matthew 28:19, ESV).

God Walks Quietly

Ron was preaching at a county church, which I recorded. The next week we were asked to send a DVD of his preaching. I wouldn't have had the DVD except God knew we were going to need it. Then the next week we were asked to come and preach at a church, where else back in Texas. We showed up, and they loved his word, so they called him back and by the next week they voted him in as pastor. So twelve weeks later, Ron is not only the senior pastor of a church, but I get to work with the youth. Now, how is that for God moving?

God continually draws us, but in my case, it pretty much stops me dead in my tracks, and firmly speaks, so that I will listen. Here is where the RV comes in. We are able to stay in our RV since the parsonage is occupied. They had a pad made just for our RV, so we could be close to the church—it was right outside the fellowship hall. As we had our first women's conference, we picked up one of our speakers at the airport. Then we took her to Red Lobster, which was her favorite restaurant. We didn't know, but God did. We got to visit and share with her all that was going on in the church. As she opened up and shared with us, we found out she had been cheated out of many things, including a car deal.

I got out my pen and wrote on the napkin to Ron. We are supposed to give her that car. Ron looked at me and said, "yeah I know." We slid the napkin over to her and she was confused. We then said see that car we picked you up in? She shook her head, yes. "Well, God told us that you are the one we are supposed to give it to. We knew we got it, but we're not sure why until now."

She said, "I can't do that."

We told her you are not going to rob us of our blessing. Honestly it's yours, when you get ready to go back home you can take it with you."

Now we see the bigger picture. We are so honored to serve such an amazing God that he would walk through our lives and put people, places, and things in order to be able to bless you and others. God loves us just that much. Pay attention. God is doing the same thing in your life every day. He desires that you get to know him as intimately as he knows you. As you pay attention, you will see God walks quietly through your life.

Women Wanting

We were having a women's conference at our church, and we were trying as hard and we could to get a lot of women involved. Our associate pastor came up to me and asked me to call his wife Audrey and invite her. I thought nothing about it, but it was a big deal for him. She grew up a Catholic, and when they married she didn't really go to church. He was a different religion than her. As I called her, I asked her if she wouldn't mind helping me out with setting up the different tables, and passing out welcome bags as the women came in. She was hooked. I didn't know at the time that she loved to do for others, so this was right up her alley. Her husband was overjoyed that she was coming to the conference.

The conference was very intimate with around fifty people attending. I had Audrey sitting by me. She said she was nervous about attending, so I kept her close. The speakers talked about how intimate God wants to be in your life. Audrey was listening intently, and I could tell she was being drawn, but she fought it.

Then Saturday morning came and one of the speakers came over to her and said something to her. She started to cry. I found out later that the speaker told her that God has a plan for her life, and it would begin this weekend. We came together after lunch and began more studies. We took a break and came back together at 6:00 p.m. I had to move to get something during the service, and I wasn't sitting as close to Audrey as I was before. I wasn't supposed to, God was dealing with her in only a way he could. Within fifteen minutes of the conference starting, she was in tears. I waited until God directed me, then I went over to talk to her. I asked why she was crying. She said because I know God wants me. I don't know what to do, I'm scared and nervous.

I told her that is the Holy Spirit drawing you. He wants your heart and life. Would you like to know Jesus like a friend? We talked and as we did she was crying even more. It was then and there she surrendered to God. She bowed her head and prayed and invited Jesus into her life. She finally was at peace. She finally quit fighting, and she finally knew God.

After the service she went up to her husband and shared with him her decision. He grabbed her and hugged her so tightly and smiled as tears ran down his face. They had been married for twenty years, and they were never on the same page when it came to God, until now. Audrey began to teach Sunday school and help with the youth.

She became a pastor's wife, supportive, loving, and involved. She didn't know it, but within months her husband would take over as the pastor for the church. The church was too small to have a full-time pastor. She stepped up and helped as secretary and example to the women in her church. Imagine, if you can, all the prayers that went up for her from her husband. With all the years of sharing the Bible, and the countless times God tried to draw her, God never quit on her.

He had too many people depending on her and what she needed to do for the kingdom of God. A husband prayers were answered, lives were changed. Thank you, God, for Audrey and her new life…surrendered, devoted, and totally in love with YOU.

Pray for Peace

We were visiting our son Michael and his wife Ashley in Oklahoma. Michael invited us in and showed us the new chairs he got at a great deal. He began sharing how he was sitting in the chair the other night with the blanket around him and his socks on. He fell asleep, but when he woke up his blanket was on the floor across the room and his socks thrown on the couch.

One time he was sitting watching TV, when he looked over between the entrances to the kitchen, there was a figure standing there. He quickly looked away and looked back and it was gone. Then in the bedroom at the back of the house, there was a picture they would hang up in the middle of the wall. Every time they would hang the picture up, the picture would be knocked down, or in the middle of the room. If they left the door open when they came back it was closed. If they left it closed it would be open.

One night they heard someone knocking on the door from the garage to the house. Then moments later they heard the door slam open. When Michael went to check on it he found nothing. So he dead bolted the door. It happened again and again. Each time they checked, there was nothing there. Then one night their dog was lying in bed with them, when all of a sudden, the dog looks up at the ceiling. Micley the dog, eyes are following something that was on Michael's side of the bed to Ashley's side of the bed. As it gets close to Ashley, the dog begins to growl. It was then that something went up. The dog's head moved to everything it was doing. Before we left we prayed over that house, since it was the house that the kids grew up in.

When I told Michelle about what had happened, she informed me that she had some similar experiences. She told me that when she was a kid she hated going to sleep in the back bedroom, because she would see hundreds of eyes looking at her. She would cover her head and pray all night long. Those eyes never did anything, but look at her, but even as a child she was rebuking them. Have you ever felt like something was watching you and trying to scare you? This place had no good memories for me while I was married. There was lots of fighting, as well as slamming doors, even at times being locked out of the house. There was more that went on, but not important as knowing that we had the power, and authority to rebuke each, and everything else that isn't of God.

Looking back, I feel like as long as we lived there we were holding back the evil that wanted to be there. Once Ashley accepted Jesus as her Savior they had no one to mess with. As we prayed and cast out the spirit in Jesus name, the house calmed down. They said the next time they visited there was nothing, like it was peaceful there. Thank you, God, that as we are full of you there is nothing put peace, love, and joy. Evil has no place in our life, unless we allow it. Help us Father to live each day full of you, so evil has no place to reside.

"Submit yourselves therefore to God. Resist the devil, and he will flee from you" (James 4:7, esv).

Unto Others

When I was first married, we moved next door to a girl named Donna. It proved to be a true lasting friendship. We all have people that become instant friends when you meet. Even though you move away you still stay in contact with them, because they speak life into you, and bless you. Donna seemed to be in the same situations as me, crazy! I think we joined forces just to be able to cope. There is nothing she wouldn't do for me. She helped watch my kids, cooked for me, and was a shoulder to cry on, more times than I care to tell. We worked at the airport together and managed to touch base from time to time.

When I moved from Oklahoma to Texas, we lost touch, but I still thought of her as a dear friend. Fate stepped in one day twenty years later. Donna was in a restaurant and saw her dad's best friend and knew that he was dating my mom. She asked for my number and he gave it to her. It wasn't soon after that I get a call saying do you remember me? Of course, I was so excited and thrilled that I finally connected up with her. We talked almost every day and I love hearing how well she was doing.

She had gone through a rough patch and was trying to find a place to stay. As we began to pray about her circumstances, God moved. She got a wonderful job, and then out of nowhere her boss gave her a new car. Next, they helped her purchase a new home.

Now, in this world, there is no one I know that deserves blessings more. She will give you everything she has, that's why God chooses to bless her. She shares her home with total strangers, when the tornado came through Moore, Oklahoma she was out feeding people that had nothing. Offering to help in any way she can. I choose to surround myself with such wonderful people because they show you Jesus everyday! I'm in awe that God shares them with me. Thank you, Father, for sharing your amazing people with me. These amazing people lead by example and as your word says, that when you've done it to the least of these you've done it unto me. Thank you, Father, for giving me another example of Jesus. The world is a better place because of them.

"And the King will answer them, Truly, I say to you, as you did it to one of the least of these my brothers, you did it to me" (Matthew 25:40, ESV).

Just Kids Being Kids

Kid: Thank you for God! (END)

Kid: I'm sorry for breaking your cord.

Me: I know that's okay!

Kid: I will get my money and pay for it.

Me: No, that's okay. You said you were sorry, and that's enough!

Kid: Sometimes, it's not. (END)

Kid: Sorry for getting mad.

Me: What made you say you're sorry?

Kid: God showed me that I needed to be sorry. (END)

Kid: It stopped raining.

Me: Yeah.

Kid: God did that.

Me: Is that right?

Kid: Yeah, cause he is awesome like that! (END)

Kid: We prayed that God would help us.

Me: What about?

Kid: This big kid wouldn't hurt us.

Me: What happened?

Kid: Then he got called inside.

Me: Is that right?

Kid: God saved us. (END)

Kid: Read me the BIG Bible tonight…

Me: You sure you are going to understand it?

Kid: It's God's word, and that's enough. (END)

Kid: I came out to be social.

Me: Really, what are you doing?

Kid: I'm playing solitaire. (END)

Bowing to pray

Kid: Thank you for Jesus!

Kid: And that he is more powerful than Ron. (END)

Determined Devotion

I met Erik when he first came to church. It was Michelle and his first date. He was very polite, kind, and he has a smile that lights up a room. It was the first time he had come to the church, so he didn't know what to expect. He hung onto every word. After three weeks, we saw Erik on a regular basis. He would come over to the house and didn't miss a service. Erik and Michelle were inseparable. Their birthdays were three days apart. They both had lost over a hundred pounds. They both were very intelligent. In fact, Erik was studying cancer research. One Sunday at the church, he walked down the aisle and accepted Jesus as his savior. Erik said he believed in God, but he really didn't have a close relationship with him. Erik's life was perfect in every way. He adored Michelle and was sure this was the girl God had for him.

While at school one day, he found out that his work was being compromised. The people at the university were treating him poorly and it was not conducive to work there any more so he left. He had nowhere to live, no money, and Michelle was fixing to move. Michelle was working as our associate in Nebraska, but we felt God calling us to another campus. We received a call from a place in California, the money was excellent and we didn't work weekends. Michelle and Erik said they could stay with us until he took another position. Erik began applying to Stanford which was fifteen minutes away.

As we took the job, it wasn't at all what we thought it was. We were on 24/7 and we couldn't speak about Jesus. The paperwork was insane. We quickly called the first campus and asked if the position was available. Of course, it was because God was teaching us a lesson. It isn't always about the money. We went from Nebraska to California and then to Mississippi. This left Erik not knowing where to go. Erik was without a job since March, and it was now June. He came for a visit in June and two weeks later had an interview with Texas A&M.

It was at this time that Erik called me and asked me to pray with him before he went to the interview. We prayed that he would have the words to say, and favor with everyone he spoke to. The interview went well, but he wouldn't know anything for a couple of months. A week or so went by, and I was prompted by God to pray for Erik. I continued to pray that God would be first in his life and that he would focus on him instead of everything else.

When I shared that with Erik he received it well. I reminded him that as the Israelites waited on God; God was with them directing their steps all the time. At this time you need to trust that God is going to take you where you are supposed to be. Then out of the blue I get a text from Erik saying that it doesn't matter where God takes him, he will trust God will all his heart. Erik was going to praise God no matter what happened. It blew me away, because just weeks ago he was worried and nervous about his decisions. We must have prayed four or five times during this process. Each prayer was different and more focused. Erik was walking closer to God than ever. He was at peace with God's purpose for his life.

Two weeks later, while he was at his parents' house in Ohio, he got an e-mail saying he had been accepted and awarded the highest fellowship offered. Erik called me saying thank you, Jesus! Shaking and excited he was crying over what God had done. There were over five hundred applicants and each one more impressive. But God saw Erik's heart and knew he would serve him well. Once again God, a work fired unjustly, no place to live, no one to turn to. So he turns to God his only hope and help. So God rewarded him with a new job, more money, close to Michelle, and more importantly a new relationship with his Heavenly Father. Only God knows the plans he has for this young man, but they are GOOD!

Go and Share

Michelle called and shared with me an experience that happened to her. She said she was straightening her spare bedroom and organizing some books. Michelle said she tossed one book at her dresser, and the book should have missed, and hit the floor. However, the book floated to the dresser and landed upright with the book pages facing her.

The book had been placed right in the middle of all of the other books on the dresser. The book was called *365 Days With Jesus*. Michelle called me, and shared what happened to her. Michelle was blown away at what she just witnessed.

A few days later I was sitting on my couch thinking about the book, and how God moved around her. As I looked up there was a small box about the size of a bandage box sitting on the TV stand. The box rocked back and forth four or five times, and then just stopped.

I smiled and said, "thank you Jesus for always moving around me too."

Only moments later, I was reminded about Ron's school issues. I needed to follow-up on Ron's student loans being consolidated. Nowadays, there are so many scams that when something good happens, you sometimes questioned whether it's real or not. As I called I found out that the loan had been consolidated and our payments would be $1070.00. Now this is crazy, so Ron calls, and resubmits the forms and they come down to $320.00.

Thank you Jesus, the payment is very manageable. It's just like God, not be outdone, God does one even better. We find out that if we file separately on our taxes the payment will be $85.00. Blessings don't stop there. Ron has several classes left to finish getting his degree, but we haven't had the money to get him back in school. After they consolidate the loans money opens up for him to be able to go back to school. Seriously every class will be paid for. Now, if you can wrap your mind around this. We paid $1000 to get into this program, which we thought might be a scam.

Then we got our payments lowered to pay back the loan. We now are able for Ron to go back to school. The $1000 that we invested was given back to us, because our payments should have been $1070, now they will be $85.

As long as Ron is in school, the payments to the student loan are deferred. We also have enough money now to finish paying for my book to be published. It all started with God showing me he was moving even with a little box. As if that wasn't enough, I was listening to God's word. Jesus is telling a man he has just healed to "Go home to your friends and tell them how much the Lord has done for you, and how he has had mercy on you."

Those words resounded in my spirit; Go tell what Jesus has done for you! I get it, the only reason I still have breath in my body, is to share what Jesus has done for me. Thank you God that every day I get to share the amazing love, incredible stories and supernatural ways you move in my life. I am in awe of YOU!

Thank You, Family

I have watch Michael grow up. He has shown kindness, love, and value to everyone around him. He cherishes his time and gives his undivided attention to whomever he is with. Growing up, he didn't have the best of circumstances, but it never kept him down. He always found the good in everything. His spirit was drawing everyone around him. It gave him opportunities to share Jesus, and let those people fall in love with him as well. His heart was always to invite them in and give them a taste of what he had. He has always had the Holy Spirit's drawing on his life and yielded to every calling.

I'm so grateful for my wonderful son whose unconditional love for God has blessed so many. He has never met a stranger, is outgoing, and honest to a fault. Michael's greatest gift is his love for the *Lord* and serving him with his whole heart. Thank you, God, for a pure heart, love for others, and for YOU. Isn't that what we are all called to do?

Michelle is a go-getter in every way. If she sees something, she has the drive and determination to go get it. God's favor and call is on her life. It was seen even as a small child. She knows that God is calling her into something even more amazing, which makes Michelle's calling more immediate. One thing she values is that she can handle her bills. As an accountant she always saves for a rainy day. She took an accountant's job even though she doesn't make enough to make ends meet. It doesn't change the fact that she tithes faithfully, because she settled that decision a long time ago, who is the most important in her life…JESUS!

She saved one time to buy a well for people in India. They have to walk sometimes ten miles to get clean water, and when they do, they are also given the living water. (God's word) She wanted to make a difference elsewhere. Making a difference comes easy to her, because that is what she has done with her whole life. She is devoted, dedicated, and desires to give God her best. Wouldn't we all do well to serve God and others to make a difference? Thank you, God, for the difference Michelle has made in my life, and for the difference she and I are going to make in others.

God has been so good to me; I serve with a tireless man of God. Ron is devoted to pleasing God and then me. I have never met a more generous man. He inspires me, and encourages me to share my faith and my stories with others. If it weren't for him, I wouldn't have written this book. Even though God kept nudging me for years, I never yielded to it. I thought

I wasn't good enough, and didn't have the education or the intelligence to pull it off. God knew Ron could speak into my life and lead by example. Ron has gone to school gotten two masters degrees and working on his PhD.

If Ron thought I was talented enough to do it, then it must be so. Ron has always spoken life into me. Sharing, as well as drawing me to have a more intimate relationship with God, which has been invaluable in my life. Ron loves without limits and has a heart for God. Which means because he knows love, he knows how to love.

Thank you God for my wonderful helpmate and friend I get to share in this life with. P.S. the pictures in the book, Ron drew most of them, and I did some, because once again he told me I could do it. In my life, God has always been there, guiding me through tough times and good times, always making them better. We make choices that determine what will happen in our lives. God steps in and tries to make our situations better.

Imagine if we would just ask God ahead of time, what we should do, what a difference our lives would be? We all try and blame God for the bad things, but reality says we live in a sinful world and bad things are going to happen. How we choose to react to them will make the difference of depending on God or ourselves.

In my life I have come to trust, lean, and depend on God to get me through. He has never disappointed me. I just wonder if you decide to give God a chance, how your life would be? In my house it's simple. As for me and my house, we choose to serve The Lord. God made people for his pleasure and the earth for ours, all of this and heaven too!

Thank you for taking the time to read my short stories. They are all based on true stories. My hope and prayer is that as you witness God moving on one person's behalf that you would stop and recognize that he does that for you too. He never stops. He is relentless at pursuing you. God loves you so much that he does everything he can to reach you right where you are. He will talk to you in a way that you can understand.

God pours into your life from the moment you are born. God wants a relationship with you. What that relationship will be is up to you. He is already here; all you have to do is reach out and ask. You have heard your whole life that you need to accept Jesus as your personal savior.

"For all have sinned and fall short of the glory of God" (Romans 3:23, ASV).

—Admit that you are a sinner.

"The wages of sin is death" (Romans 6:23a, ASV).

—Understand that you deserve to die for your all your sins.

"But the gift of God is eternal life through Jesus Christ our Lord" (Romans 6:23b, ASV).

—It's a free gift you can't earn it, but he wants to give it to you.

"God demonstrates his own love for us, in that while we were yet sinners Christ died for us" (Romans 5:8, ASV).

—Jesus died for you knowing all that you did; he still took your place. God loves you!

"Whoever will call on the name of the Lord will be saved!" (Romans 10:13, ASV)

—Jesus I invite you into my life!

"If you confess with your mouth Jesus as Lord, and believe in your heart that God raised Jesus from the dead, you shall be saved; for with the heart man believes, resulting in righteousness, and with the mouth he confesses, resulting in salvation" (Romans 10: 9,10, ASV).

Let me explain for a moment so you might understand what these scriptures mean? From the time you are two or three, you begin to do things wrong (SIN). Imagine that you carry a bag with you, and every time you sin you add to the bag.

For example: Tell a lie; throw it in the bag, steal something; throw it in the bag, hate someone; throw it in the bag, disobey your mom or dad; throw it in the bag. You get the idea? So from the time you were two or three until however old you are now you have a lot of (SINS). Now, I don't know about you, but I have messed up a lot. My bag full of (SINS) is as big as a house.

Here is where Jesus comes in. God is in heaven and he looks at his perfect son and says. They don't know how to live this life right. You go down there and show them. Jesus could have said no way, but he loved you so much He left heaven to be a perfect example. He was tempted in every way we were but he NEVER sinned. Now Jesus knew that not only would he have to live a perfect life, but also he would have to die for you.

Knowing you had no way to get to heaven, Jesus became that bridge between heaven and earth. You can't cross over unless you ask. You see, Jesus went to the cross and while he was dying he looked at your (SIN) and said, you weren't meant to carry that, give it to me. The bag of (SIN) that you carry is too hard to deal with. Jesus asks you to give it to him. You were never meant to carry that heavy load of (SIN). You do have to do one thing though; you have to ask him to take it. It's like having a candy bar—you want it, but you can't have it until you ask for it. If you are tired of carrying all of the bad things you have done your whole life, then you can ask Jesus to take it from you.

Here's the neat thing, He will take it and toss it as far as heaven is from earth and remember it no more. That's right your (SINS) are gone, and remembered no more. He doesn't hold your past against you. He gives you a new start—fresh and clean walking with him. Now, that you asked Jesus to remove your bag (SINS) your heart is clean. That is where Jesus can come and live. He helps you make good choices because he lives in you. So every day you can choose to live a life pleasing to him. Then the relationship you have with God will begin because he knows Jesus is living in you. You are probably wondering why he would do this for me. God always wanted a life with you but (SIN) separated us from him.

God is perfect and has no (SIN) around him. That's why Jesus had to come and live in us, so it shows God that (SIN) doesn't live in us anymore. Here is the question: Would you like to know if you are forgiven, and like a new start on this life that we messed up? Then all you have to do is pray this prayer.

It's you talking to God, getting real, honest before him. But until you ask you can't receive his free gift of *salvation* (Saved from your SINS). Pray this prayer if you know you would like to receive Jesus into your heart; it's your choice.

Dear Heavenly Father, I know I'm a sinner. I know Jesus came and led a perfect life. Forgive me of my SINS. Come into my heart and be *The Lord* (BOSS) of my life. Thank you for saving me. In Jesus name, Amen!

Wow, you did it. Angels are rejoicing throwing a party because one soul is saved. Congratulations, it's the greatest decision you will ever make. I'm so very proud of you and happy for your new life in Christ. You see we are born in the flesh once and born in the spirit once. Once you accepted Jesus, you were adopted into his family. You have a home in heaven, and no one can snatch you out of it. You're Jesus's for life!

Every day when you get up you need to ask God what is it that he would like you to do. Then go do it. Walk with him, he will show you all of this and heaven too. God loves you so much he sent his son to take your place. Now that you're his son or daughter you live for him. I know you will make him proud, you already do.

There's one last thing—Tell someone what you did. Share with anyone and everyone what Jesus did for you. I know I wouldn't want anyone to not have a home in heaven because I didn't tell them. Besides that, look at all the cool stuff they miss out on because they didn't walk with God.

You get one chance at life, and you might as well get it right the first time. If you would like to share your decision with me, I would be so happy to hear from you. Wearjesuswell@yahoo.com is where you can contact me. I will pray with you and celebrate your new life. Imagine one more added to the kingdom of heaven. I can't wait to talk you and neither can GOD!